*I am the shadow, I am the light,*
*I am the tree, I am the seed,*
*I am the dewdrop, I am the ocean*
*I am the heartbeat, I am the silence,*
*I am the dragon, I am the dragonfly,*
*I am the fire, I am the spark,*
*I am the mist, I am the mountain,*
*I am the flute, I am the song,*
*I am wisdom, I am ignorance,*
*I am the boundless, I am the bound,*
*I am death, I am life...*
*Above all, I am.*

POPULAR PRAKASHAN PVT LTD
35-C, Pt. Madan Mohan Malaviya Marg
Tardeo, Mumbai 400 034

© SATISH GUPTA, 2005
5, Tolstoy Marg, New Delhi-110001, India
Telephone: (+91-11) 23314806, 23725290
Email: satamita@vsnl.com
www.satishgupta.com

(4021)
ISBN - 81-7991-273-6

*Edited by*
Anupa Mehta

*Design*
Spirit Designs Pvt Ltd

*Typeset in Rotis*

*Printed by*
Saurabh Printers (P) Ltd

*Published by*
Ramdas Bhatkal for
Popular Prakashan Pvt Ltd
35-C, Pt. Madan Mohan Malaviya Marg,
Tardeo, Mumbai 400 034.

I am the dewdrop,
I am the ocean...

For Ananda
*Who needs no knowing*

Zen Stories, Haikus and Reflections
SATISH GUPTA


*Foreword by His Holiness, the Dalai Lama*

# Contents

## Streaming Daylight
*Thoughts and Ruminations*     17

    The Wizard     19
    Judgment     21
    Wealth     22
    Power     23
    Duality     24
    Barriers     25
    Horizon     28
    No Action     30
    Awareness     31
    Thinking     33
    Insight     34
    Unheard Sound     36
    Transformation     38
    The Wheel     40
    Spirituality     43
    Journey     44
    Satori     45
    Web     48

## Drifting Clouds
*Haiku and Brushwork*     51

## Still Waters
*Incidents and Anecdotes*   81

    Ascent   82
    Possession   84
    Deceit   86
    Nomad   88
    Sharing   90
    Aesthete   91
    Secret   96
    Appearance   102
    Silence   105
    Prison   107
    Habit   109
    Winning and Losing   111
    Nothingness   112
    Rebellion   113
    The Jewel   116
    The Great Wall   119
    Perfection   120
    Enough   122
    Exhale   126

## Fleeting Moments
*Insights and Reflections*   131

**THE DALAI LAMA**

Satish Gupta is a poet, sculptor and painter who gives vivid expression to his rich imagination. As a contemporary artist with firm roots in India's rich and ancient culture, he has also found creative and personal inspiration in the artistic genius of Zen Buddhism.

I am happy to know that in conjunction with the opening of an exhibition of a selection of his paintings on Buddhist themes, he is releasing a book of poems entitled, *I am the Dewdrop, I am the Ocean.* The very words of the title remind me that just as the dewdrop, being water, shares many qualities with the ocean, so do each of us as individual human beings share with the ocean-like array of other human beings, not only the desire for freedom, peace and happiness, but also the potential and right to secure them. Moreover, this common right and aspiration is the reason why I believe it is good if we can all help each other however and whenever we can.

THE DALAI LAMA
October 31, 2005

# Spirits Enriched

As a surgeon, mine is a world of science, a physical world that relies on demonstrable facts. In the winter of 1994, a new mystical force converged with my universe. Satish Gupta, a man of art, spirituality and compassion cast a new light on our souls. In the ensuing time, Satish and his family fused with ours; his paintings, sculpture, prose and poetry have opened our consciousness to make space for a broader experience of Life.

This publication, *I am the dewdrop, I am the ocean*, is a collection of his meditations, reflections, and Haikus which flow from decades of his life experience and observations. Sitting with them in silence is like being at the foot of the master: our receptivity has been expanded, our spirits enriched, and we are blessed to enjoy a sense of peace that Satish's creative beauty brings to our lives.


JOHN M. TEW, Jr. MD
*FACS, FRCS Edinburgh*
*Professor of Neurosurgery*
*University of Cincinnati*

---

*Dr John M. Tew, Jr. MD operated upon Satish Gupta*
*for a brain tumor in the winter of 1994, in Cincinnati.*

*Snowflakes  
on a winter morning  
– my life floating*

Cincinnati, Winter 1994

# Introduction

The yin and the yang, the negative black, and the positive white, are essential to the Universe. When they are in balance, they transcend duality to become one — or the empty circle, *shunya*.

Black and white: falsehood and truth. Though there are many shades of grey in between, each is as valid as the other: with reasoning, we can justify anything.

But, Zen is not about logic. It goes beyond.

When we let spirit take over, when we begin to trust our instincts, the essential truth becomes clear - as clear as black and white; bringing us a step closer to Buddha.

I have written these reflections and stories intuitively, drawing only from the forms of Zen tradition. Though born a Hindu, I am drawn to Zen Buddhism — as an artist, I am enamoured by its aesthetics. I love the emptiness in the calligraphic works of Zen masters, their use of asymmetry, simplicity, and, above all, the silence. Zen philosophy provides inspiration — I feel an affinity to the form and the silence, which match my way of thinking.

Over the years, travelling to Buddhist sites of worship, such as Nepal, Ladakh, Sikkim, Bhutan, Sri Lanka, Thailand and Japan, I observed and experienced several Buddhist traditions and practices - from herein emerged the concept of the 'roshi'. The 'roshi' could easily be a *yogi* or a rishi - in this book I also refer to him as 'grand master' or 'wise one,' a being who intrigues and enlightens. He does not belong to any sect. He simply is.

The haikus were written in different places over a span of 25 years. In many, I have moved away from the traditional seventeen syllable/three line format. I have tried however to keep alive the spirit of the form.

If read by silencing the logical mind this volume may yield something beautiful...triggering thought processes that might allow deeper insights into everyday life, the seemingly mundane.

SATISH GUPTA
*New Delhi, India,*
*Autumn 2005*

# Streaming Daylight

*Thoughts and Ruminations*

# The Wizard

With a wave of his glistening magic wand, the wizard wove a thousand dreams – one for you, one for me and one for anyone who might crave a dream.

It was a splendid day among the undulating dunes which merged into a sequined night. The wizard lifted his shining wand and waved it at the caravan beyond. 'Do you need a dream? An exotic dream to lighten the burden of all the weight you carry? Do you need a dream to listen once again to the drumbeats of your heart? Do you need a dream to turn the caterpillar into a butterfly?'

'Yes, yes,' replied the samurai, 'I want a dream to conquer and rule the world, a dream that will make me the emperor of the universe, a dream in which I control everything.'

'Granted,' said the wizard, adding, 'but there's a small price to pay. I will make you emperor of the world…only you will have to conquer one little thing.'

'I will do anything to become the ruler of the universe. Tell me what I need to do,' said the samurai.

'Can you control your anger? Can you conquer this one little thing? If yes, I will turn you into a king…'

'Of course… I never get angry. Why, I am the most peaceful person on earth!'

The wizard waved his magic wand and there was a swirling dust devil. Everything turned round and round. When the dust settled, the samurai was enthroned on a celestial chair, golden and embedded with the beautiful stars of the universe. He uttered a command and everybody fell at his feet. His every wish turned to reality. He was in control, ruling the universe.

One evening, the samurai was seated on his throne at the top of a flight of thousands of steps, enjoying an evening of dance. The most beautiful dancers from unknown worlds were assembled for his pleasure.

As the music rose to a crescendo and the dancers swirled, a silent figure walked slowly through them. He climbed up towards the samurai, one step at a time.

Intoxicated and blinded with power, the samurai failed to recognize the intruder approaching him. The mysterious figure dared to come right up to the samurai, looked deep into his eyes, his hands on his hips and his head held high.

Furious, the samurai screamed at the top of his voice to the guards, 'Kill him! Kill him!'

The silent figure revealed his face: it was the roshi, the grand master.

Once again, there was the swirling dust devil. Momentarily blinded, the samurai struggled to open his eyes and gaze at the wizard-monk as he disappeared into the distance.

'Do you need a dream? One for you, one for me...'

# Judgment

Do we not judge all the time? What is our first reaction when we meet someone new? We ask ourselves, 'Do I like this person? No I don't like his long hair; I don't like his habit of standing on one leg; I don't even like his red shirt. Yes, his shoes are shiny...but perhaps he bought them yesterday. He couldn't possibly be polishing them everyday!'

We judge all the time – which is why we miss a lot of things, alienate people and lose touch with life.

Judging others, things, ideas and situations, only boosts our own ego. We feel superior just by passing a verdict. However, does this habit really help anything? Or us? Do we become more powerful?

Water, one of nature's most powerful elements, is non judgmental.

Therein lies its force.

# Wealth

Two very rich men were walking on a mountain path near a monastery. They were trying to impress each other with their wealth. One, wearing pearl earrings said, 'See this land that stretches to the far horizon? All of it belongs to me.'

Not to be outdone, the man in long flowing robes said, 'That's nothing, the entire mountain behind the monastery with the apple orchard belongs to me.'

As they were talking, a man came up the path in a very ostentatious chariot. He was surveying the area as he wanted to buy some land.

When he realized that the land belonged to the two men, he was delighted. He offered them sacks of gold coins to acquire their property.

A young monk, who overheard their conversation, said with a smile, 'You may buy this land, or that, but what you can't buy is the open sky because that belongs to me.'

# Power

However powerful and revered or feared a leader, an empress, an army general or even a holy man, there comes a time when power must be relinquished. Willingly. Gracefully.

This is the law of Nature.

Thunderclouds, powerful, ominous and threatening, must give up their destructive force and evaporate into beneficial rain.

If they cling to their power and refuse to dissolve, they will blow in the dark sky, hated and feared by all beneath; never loved.

In becoming beneficial rain they realize their real strength.

# Duality

Two acolytes were engaged in a heated discussion on the merits of the sutras. They had studied the ancient scriptures in depth and were arguing about the finer points.

They approached the roshi to settle their argument. One acolyte asked the teacher, 'Master aren't there 1,84,000 sentient beings in this universe? My friend insists that there are only 1,83,301. He also insists that the sacred mantra should be chanted 20,000 times during the eleventh moon. I think the number is only 19,500.'

'Very interesting,' replied the wise roshi, adding, 'but I lost count beyond one. At two all the problems begin.

'In this land of Buddha everything is one, because Buddha is in everything. Our anxieties are a result of the duality in our thinking. We see things, people and objects as separate from ourselves. When I say you, does it not include me? Can we ever differentiate? Can we ever separate things?

'Isn't the seed the same as the tree? Can we separate the water from the river, or the river from the sea? 'Where does "I" begin? Where does "I" end? What am I?

'If I eat this apple off the plate does it not become me? Or do I not become the apple? If you and I are sitting in this room and you take a breath and exhale, and I breathe in, don't you become I? Don't we inhale the same breath that Buddha exhaled thousands of years ago? We, you and I, are embodiments of the Universal Spirit. There is no duality in nature. There is just oneness.'

# Barriers

The monk was having a particularly difficult time with his meditation. He kept struggling to find a way to put his mind to rest. Each time he tried to block off a thought and concentrate on his breathing, or, whenever he tried to meditate on the pure sound of the mantra, he came up against a solid stone wall.

He kept pushing it aside, but the dark wall would not go away. He tried to imagine the light beyond, a beautiful primal lake, with moonlight falling gently on the lapping waves, but the wall facing him was so thick and dense that he could not shatter it. He could not dismantle it.

He thought, 'Perhaps, if I concentrate hard enough and break the wall, stone by stone, I could clear it.' With each breath he tried to remove one stone at a time. As soon as he removed one stone, another appeared in its place. It was almost as if an unseen mason was building the wall faster than the monk could dismantle it.

'It has always been like this with me. Why do I always come up against barriers in my path? Right from childhood there have been obstacles. How hard I tried to study, yes and even getting into the monastery was torturous. Didn't I sit at the doorstep with my head bent down, my back aching for weeks without moving, before the roshi accepted me as a disciple?'

'I am strong. I will clear everything in my way...' He flexed his muscles, struggled hard, and kept pushing the wall away, yet he was unable to make it budge. Exhausted, the monk fell down and gave up the battle. His mind became a complete blank, finally open to everything.

The wise roshi, observing the young monk through his struggle, knew that at last he was ready. He led him to his private garden of raked sand. In the middle of the garden was the empty frame of a door. The roshi made the monk walk through it, back and forth, and said to him in a deep reassuring voice, 'Just like this empty frame of a gate through which you walked effortlessly, life is a "Gateless Gate". There are no barriers in life. Buddha's world is free, the walls and the doors of ignorance are only in your mind. Do not struggle. Be one with life.'

# Horizon

'Master, where do Heaven and Earth meet? How far away am I from the horizon of enlightenment?' asked the monk.

The wise roshi replied, 'Imagine you are sailing on a vast ocean. You notice another sailboat in the distance. The wind is blowing hard. You gaze at the sailboat rushing towards the horizon where heaven and earth meet. And you say, 'Oh! The sailor is fortunate to be at that cosmic junction', unaware that he is having the same thoughts.

'You are the meeting point, because heaven and earth meet where you are. You are the Cosmic Centre. We are blessed to be the Centre. It is only when we become aware of this blessing, can we transform our lives.

'The light is never away.'

# No Action

At the beginning of the meditation session, the master told the gathered monks, 'Most of us are afraid of stillness. We think we need to constantly do something. Look around and you will see us adjust our robes, or check whether fellow monks are sitting in the correct posture. You will notice that we tend to fidget, let our eyes wander into the distance, as if to see if the sun has set!

'Ceaseless activity is like a drug, required by our body to keep it on a permanent high. But if we can get rid of it, life could be very different. What I am referring to is no-action, which is not to be confused with inaction. It is not laziness; it is a state of being, a state of being still. This is called *mushin*. Many of our mundane actions are a waste of energy. It is very difficult to be still. Like a rock in the ocean, with a turbulent sea hitting it constantly, eroding it bit by bit. Ultimately, the sea weathers away the rock. Nevertheless, the stoic rock emanates power and strength in its stillness. And when its function is over, the rock turns, once more, into boundless sand. Be like the rock.'

# Awareness

A young man, who had lost his parents in an earthquake, his home and almost everything he ever had, decided to become a monk.

He searched far and wide till he came across a monastery on a hill overlooking a river. He was accepted into the monastery as a student since the master saw that he needed spiritual succour.

To strengthen his spirit and body, the young man was put though a gruelling regimen. His regimen began at three in the morning with a cup of green tea, a bath and then a session of meditation till dawn. This was followed by a simple meal of soup and rice, work in the garden for a few hours, then off to study the scriptures and meditate, after which, a little rest and then to sit still for a few hours until evening. At night the young initiate would eat a simple meal and then retire to his cell for some hours of sleep.

This went on for a few months, but the young man felt that he had made no progress.

Dejected, he went to the master, who only told him to continue. In fact, the master made it even more difficult by asking him to join the monks on their daily rounds of begging in the village.

This disciplined routine continued for many months, but this time the young man was totally broken in spirit and decided to leave the monastery.

He decided to go the master to say goodbye, though unable to say that he wanted to leave.

The young man walked down the hill and sat next to the river, ready to jump into the rushing waters. Just then the master's hand appeared and touched him gently on the shoulder and said, 'Think before you jump. Life is not as bad as that. Sometimes, we think we are losers; that we have bad luck; that life has not treated us well. This is not so. Most often we are just not aware of the precious things we possess.

'See that fisherman on the river bank. I have been watching him for hours. He waits and waits and lifts his bait, finding no fish. He shakes his head in frustration. Look, look at him now. He has just pulled his net out of the river. He is utterly disappointed and angry, unaware of the treasure he has just caught – pure glistening water!'

'Your spiritual strength is just like this crystalline water.'

# Thinking

And the roshi said to the monk, who was very disturbed about the progress he was making with his meditation, 'Don't mull over the same futile thoughts. It is like washing your hands over and over. Surely if you saw me doing this you would think that I had gone mad. Cluttering our minds with useless thoughts amounts to the same.

'We create a tangled web, a prison for ourselves. We cling to thoughts as if our very identity depended on it. When, in fact, clinging to thoughts is useless. This does not mean that we turn into imbeciles or unthinking brutes. It only means that truth cannot be arrived at just by thinking. It is not an interactive process. It is just there. When we breathe we do not think that I am now going to take a breath. Or if thirsty, we do not say "now this glass of water will go down my throat and quench my thirst." We just do it.

'We must let our thoughts flow like the river, unhindered. And allow them to reflect the seven colours of the rainbow. Only then can we experience their true essence.'

# Insight

The Zen master took the monk to the edge of the sea and said, 'I want you to be silent like the sea in full storm; quiet like the volcano erupting; still like the samurai rushing into battle.'

The monk was unable to understand the roshi's strange words, but was determined to follow the master's advice.

Several days passed and he kept going back to the master with different answers. But the master kept sending him back to meditate more.

Weeks later, there was still no understanding in the monk's mind and he asked the roshi to explain.

He said, 'Well, you are only thinking of the noise the stormy sea makes. Have you not heard the silence between the waves? Does the volcano not keep still between the boom and the eruption? Isn't the samurai still before he takes a deep breath to shout and scare his enemy and rush ahead on horse-back?'

The next day the monk came back. He said, 'Last night, I heard the flower opening its petals. I heard the sound of my father opening and shutting his eyes. I heard the dewdrops falling on lotus leaves. I heard the fish swimming in the pond.'

The monk smiled and said, 'There is only one problem. Silence is overpowering. It will take getting used to.'

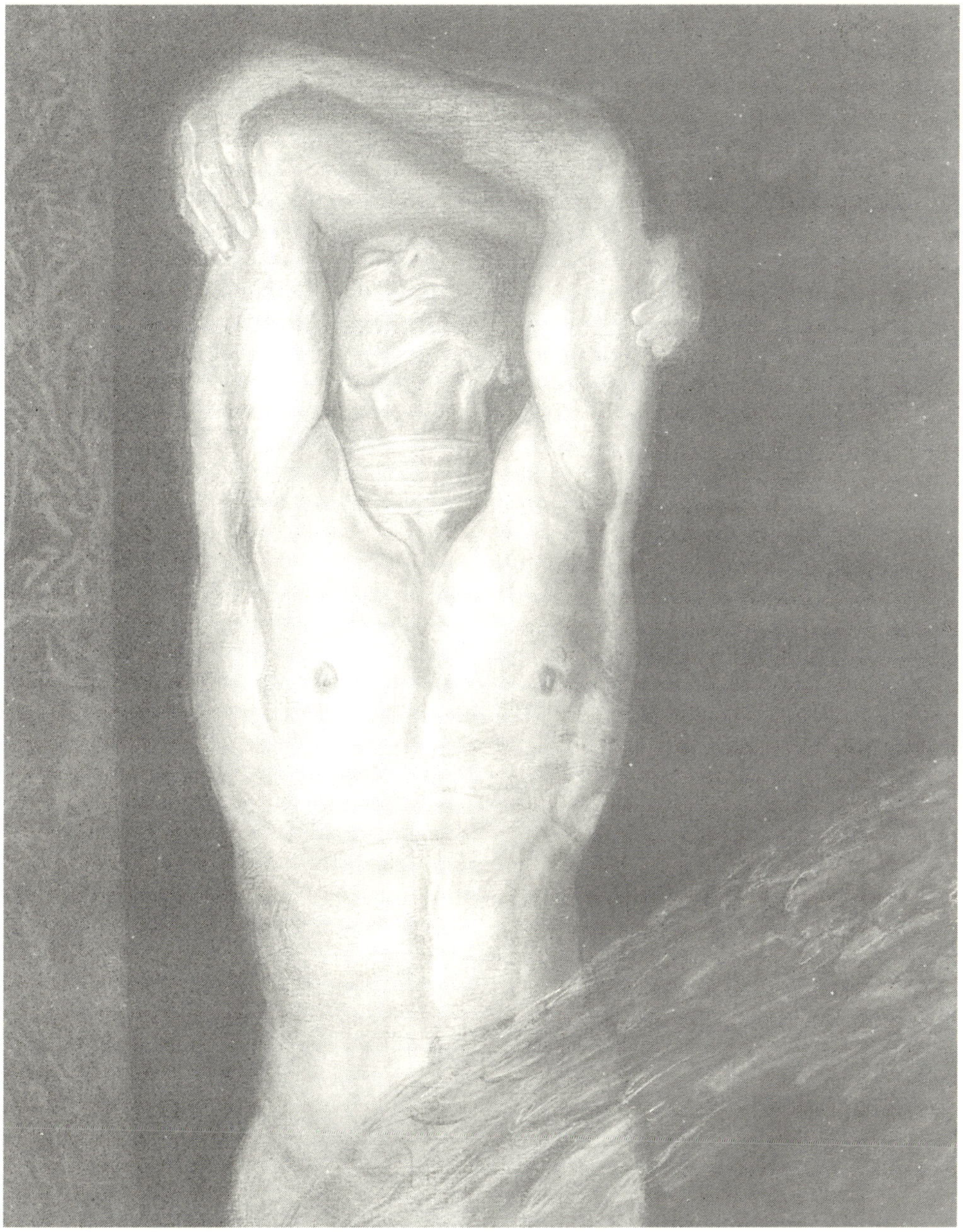

# Unheard Sound

In the dimly lit monastery, the young monk heard the sound of the prayer bells. Immediately he put his hands to his ears. He heard the other monks chanting and he brought his hands even closer to his ears. But he could only shut out the sound for a moment. The soft chanting transformed itself into the loud drums of his beating heart.

He could not accept the fact that though he had tried so hard to shed his ego and joined the monastery, desire continued to linger. His untamed self remained however much he tried to free himself from its bondage. If only he could block off desire by plugging his ears, yet be able to listen to sacred chanting. He was distraught. Years of practice had gone to waste.

Observing the futile actions of the monk, the wise roshi said, 'Let go, don't be afraid. There are always some discordant notes in a symphony. You will soon learn to listen to unheard sound, and be part of the symphony.

'The music is within you.'

37

# Transformation

It was freezing cold outside. The snow-clad mountains shivered in the wind. The first rays of sun entered the tearoom through the floor level shoji window.

The water in the teapot - it hung from an iron chain suspended from the ceiling beam - simmered. The master stirred the green tea with a bamboo whisk and took a sip to taste it before offering another cup to his honoured guest, the emperor.

'Sensei, I have conquered all. My kingdom now consists of vast territory far beyond those snow-clad mountains to where the sky meets jade waters. People shiver at the very mention of my name. I just have to raise an eyebrow and they freeze to death. My enemies work as bonded labour, slaves transforming this land for my people. I have fought great battles, sensei, to possess this immense power. I have run out of things to conquer. I need a challenge. I need a new enemy. The trouble is that they fear me so much that they surrender even before I have raised my sword, for they know that I fear nothing.'

The roshi sat quietly with his eyes half closed and nodded from time to time, listening to the emperor's monologue.

Without warning, the roshi pushed the hanging kettle towards the emperor. The boiling water spilled before it could burn his face. The roshi noticed a fleeting expression of fear on the emperor's face, before he regained his composure, and fear quickly transformed into anger.

'You needed a challenge. You needed an enemy. The new enemy is your self, which needs transformation. And as for your being fearless, I have my doubts.'

With a deep bow, the emperor lifted his silk robes and walked towards the open door. He sat cross-legged on the cold steps outside the tearoom for a long, long time.

He took deep breaths of the pure air and gazed at a lone eagle flying freely over the snow-clad mountains.

# The Wheel

After spending years in the monastery and not getting far in his practice, the young monk was about to give up hope, but he decided to go to the wise old sage one last time.

The roshi was in deep meditation. His folded hands were glowing with intense energy. The monk hesitated for a long time. At last in his despair, he dared to disturb the roshi's concentration.

'O great one, what is the meaning of my existence? What is the use of my struggling to comprehend the truth if the wheel of life keeps moving by itself? I have no control over my destiny, it is so futile, the water flows from the mountains into the sea by itself, the seasons change regularly and great stars keep spinning in the sky by themselves. I feel so insignificant. How does it matter what I do or not do? Whether I am brutal or gentle; whether I live or die... Is it not totally immaterial?

The roshi, seated on a rock near the sea, whispered softly. His voice mingled with lapping waves as his robes flew in the gentle breeze.

'Yes, you cannot hold the thunder, or stem the waterfall. You cannot stop the moon's reflection on the lapping waves. The wheel of time will turn by itself. Did you hear the sound of the rushing wave that just dissolved on the beach? Of the billions and billions of waves that have flowed through time, each one is special. There never was one like this one and there never will be another.

'Yesterday, I observed a white lily in the monastery. The plant had struggled through the stones to grow. At last there was this pristine flower that stood upright taking its rightful share of sunlight in our shaded garden. It glistened and radiated life. Today, its head has drooped. Tomorrow it will melt into nothingness and the day after, a new bud will open repeating the same process.

'Yet, the presence of that particular lily was singular, and so will the presence of the next one. Each thing, each event, each being is unique and complete as it is an intrinsic part of the great wheel. You are an indispensable cell of Buddha's body, the blood in his veins.

'It is you who make the Cosmos turn in all its glory.'

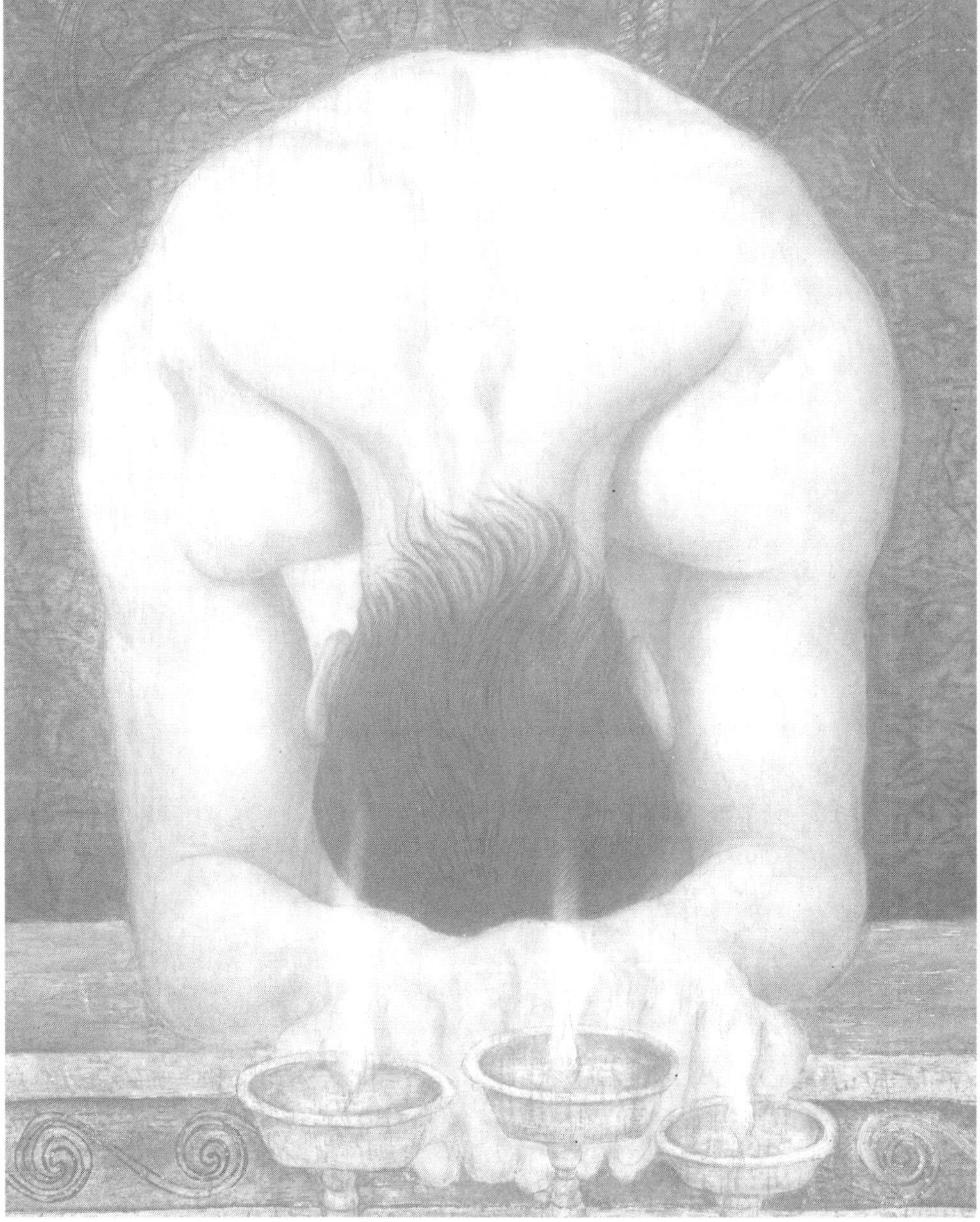

# Spirituality

And the roshi said to the monk, 'Reciting the mantras ten thousand times and memorizing the great scriptures has limited value. Fasting for long periods, burning incense, lighting butter lamps daily, though essential for your training, is not a sure path to Buddha.

'Do not wrap yourself in layers and layers of spirituality to cover your untamed ego.

'Spirituality can easily become bondage - a very comforting prison.'

# Journey

As I drift aimlessly in my boat, I watch a young man jump into the river from his boat. He flips in the air many times like a dolphin, till finally he pushes his boat to the sandy shore and anchors it near a larger one.

He wanders towards a child playing with marbles on sand, laughs and joins the game.

He goes back to the river, takes a holy dip and pushes his boat into the river again. The young man caresses his boat and climbs aboard. He continues on the journey and starts rowing. Soon he rests the oars, takes the wet cloth off his waist and stands on the edge of the boat. He holds the cloth up in the breeze to dry. It sways like a sail pushing the boat forward, one with the elements.

It is dusk. I follow him in my boat for a while. The atmosphere is magical; I listen to the mantras being chanted on the bank as the fire consumes mortal flesh and releases the soul.

I light some oil lamps and offer them to the river. They float slowly towards his (now distant) boat and into the night. They join the journey and the journeyman for whom there is no distinction: the boat and he switch roles constantly. It is amazing to see the ease with which he holds and then releases his destiny, remaining one with the flowing time.

In Tao this is called the kai-ho process. The breath comes and goes, the fist clenches and releases without a moment's hesitation. Just like this young man, who, by just being his natural self has achieved wisdom akin to that of great saints seated on the banks of an eternal river.

# Satori

In a far off monastery, there was a handsome young monk who meditated with single-minded devotion to attain satori.

He was a disciple of the wise old roshi who kept giving him koans or riddles to solve. The young monk had a great grasp of the religious texts and a vibrant, alert mind. He could, with time, unravel the mysteries of the Zen riddles for which there is no logical answer. The Zen koans are given to an acolyte to meditate upon, so as to block the mind from its logical, mundane, thought process and awaken an intuitive understanding of reality.

The roshi took a liking for the young monk and was impressed with his progress.

One day, the ecstatic monk barged into the roshi's chamber and declared that he had attained satori. The roshi, unsure of the monk's claim, tested him again and again. In the end he blessed the young disciple as he felt the monk's awakening was genuine.

Years passed, yet the roshi harboured some doubts about the monk having experienced satori.

The monk left the monastery soon after his enlightenment. In time, he became the roshi of his own sect. The handsome monk, having attained satori at such a young age became very egoistical and began leading a debauched life. He started enjoying the company of painted women, lavish food and expensive robes. He justified all this by preaching that since this whole world was Buddha, there was no good or evil, there was no right or wrong action. He did this under the shade of his satori experience.

Word of his lifestyle reached the old roshi, who became very distressed, as now, after all these years, doubts about the validity of the monk's satori experience that had lingered in his mind were confirmed.

To test him again, the roshi invited his disciple to a feast in the monastery. He knew his fondness for food and drink so he had the cook refer to old secret recipes to make exotic dishes for the feast.

The acolytes who worked hard to prepare the meal were very upset as they had heard all about the debauched monk and did not wish to entertain him. They thought their roshi had grown senile to organize such a homecoming. There were murmurs of discontent running all through the monastery.

It was dusk. The monk arrived with great fanfare, seated in a golden chariot like the emperor. He descended from his throne and sat on an embroidered cushion reserved for very special guests.

At last, the food arrived along with a rare wine. The monk was served first. Without waiting for the roshi to begin, the young monk started gorging on his food. After a few bites, he spat it out on the pristine floor. There was a hushed silence. The monks were aghast at his behaviour. The wise roshi comforted the monk who blurted out between bouts of vomit, 'Your food is so awful... it is so stale!'

After taking a bite the roshi said, 'Oh is that so? Yes, you are right. I am glad that you realized it is stale. Why, it is as stale as your satori. Just like this food, yesterday's satori won't do. It needs to be fresh like dew every moment.'

47

# Web

Having given up his sensuality, physicality, and worldliness, the samurai went to the misty mountains. He gave up everything he had, all his wealth and possessions; he tried to free himself from all attachments.

He sat in meditation for long hours, facing the great statue of Padmasambhava, lit the butter lamp and chanted the mantras for hours on end. He shaved his hair, became bald and donned a monk's robes.

Wearing the robes, he realized, was still an attachment; he was caught in a worldly web. He had to free himself of even the robes, from the fact of being a monk...for that too was a trap.

He tore off the robes in wild abandon. It was sacrilege but he felt closer to the life force, closer to the great void. He had broken free. Naked he leaped into the ephemeral, free floating clouds, high above the world.

He felt unbound, great joy. The clouds enveloped him, surrounded him with their nebulous being. Another web...

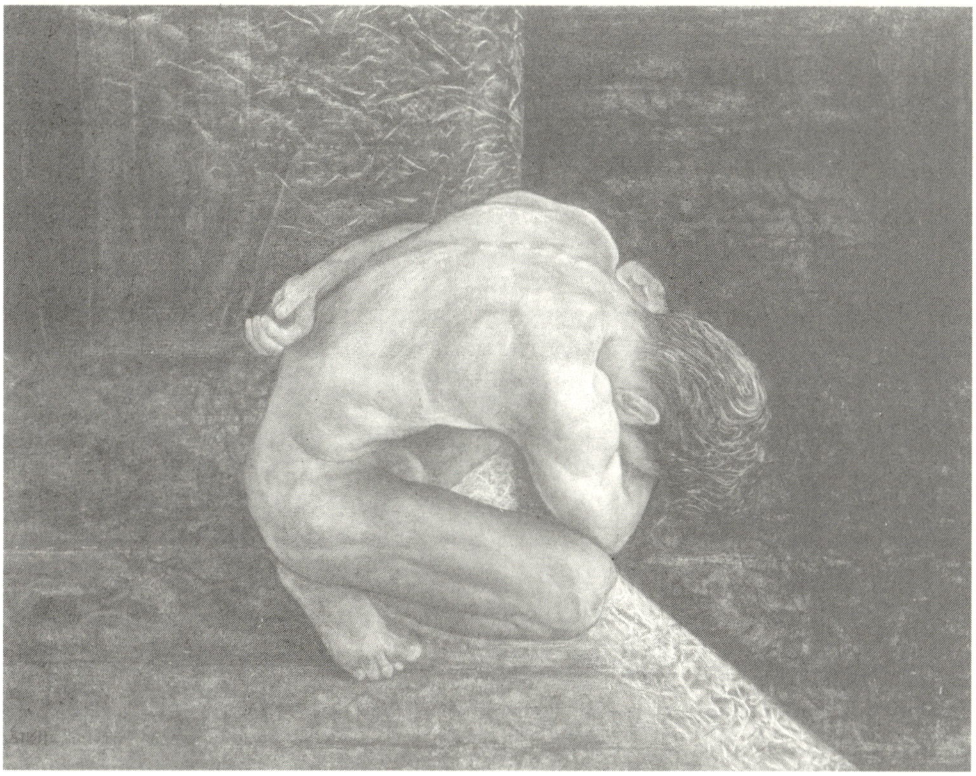

# Drifting Clouds

*Haiku and Brushwork*

*Water flowing,
no time to pass judgment
on uneven boulders*

*Rushing, roaring sea
floating over it all,
the silence filled shell*

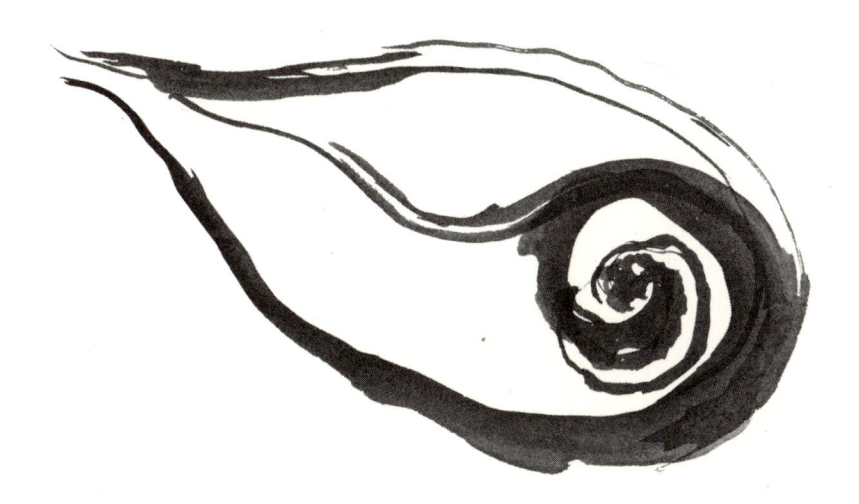

*Echoing
in silent waters
sound of
the broken wave*

*The wine
is finished
– drink more
of the sea*

*Our precious dreams,
just castles
in the sand,
— but what
treasures within*

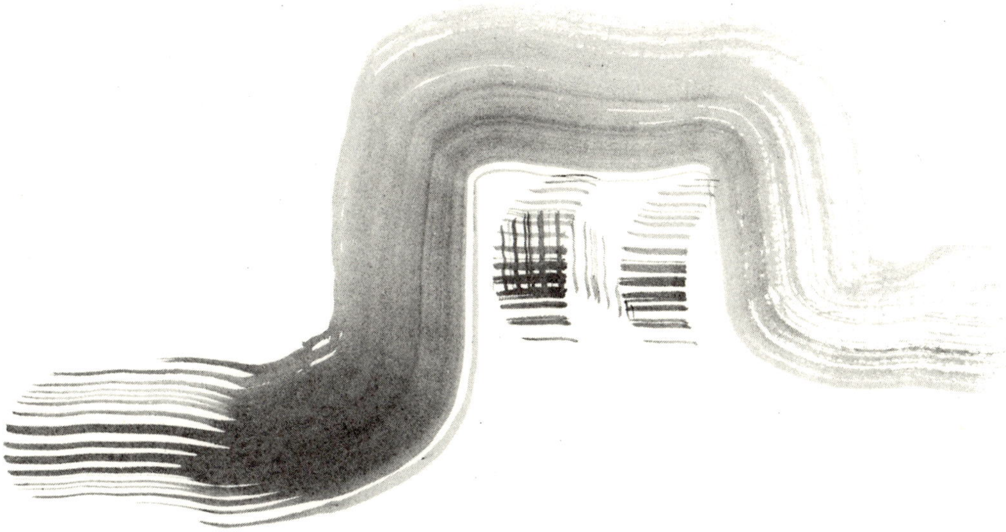

*In the amber sky,*
*a flock of wild geese*
*– the young one*
*out of step*

*Flying through
the monsoon clouds
− a silent thunder*

61

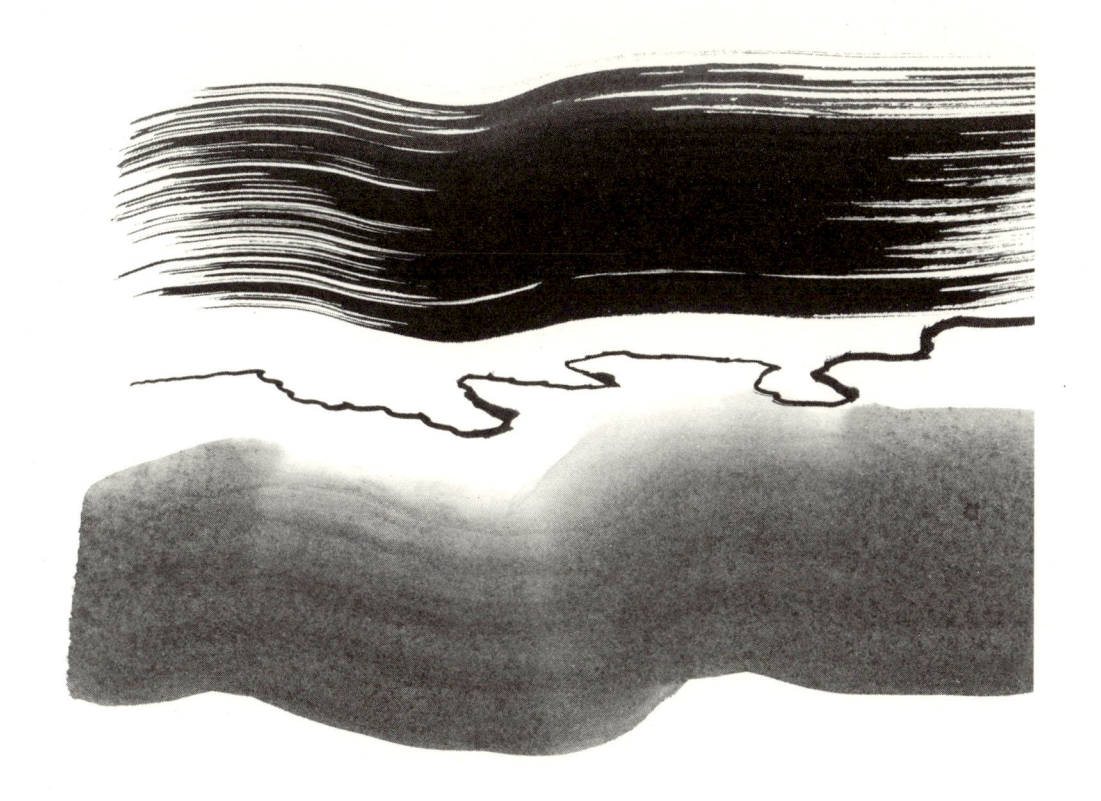

*Evidence*
*– carved in stone*
*a lover's cry*

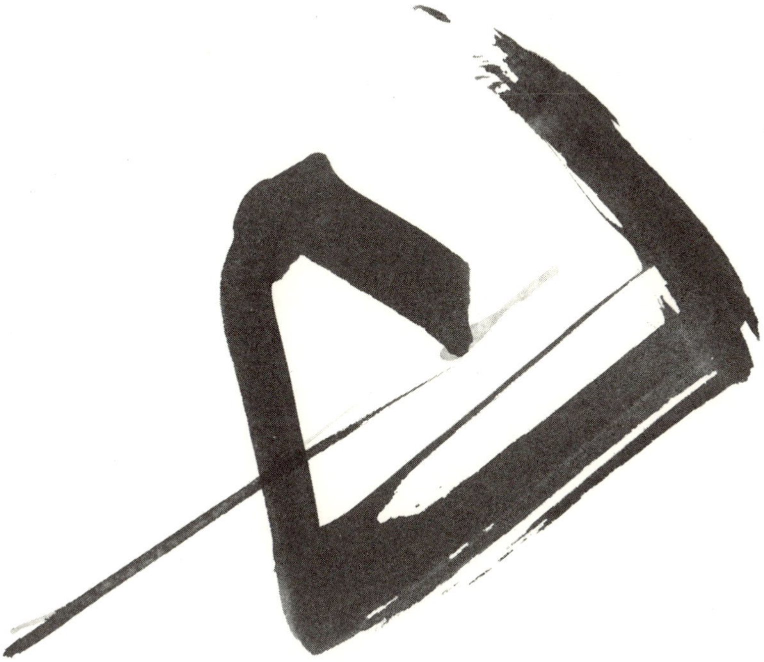

*Sieve*
*to gather*
*my thoughts*

*Storm clouds,
on the horizon,
— my sailboat nest*

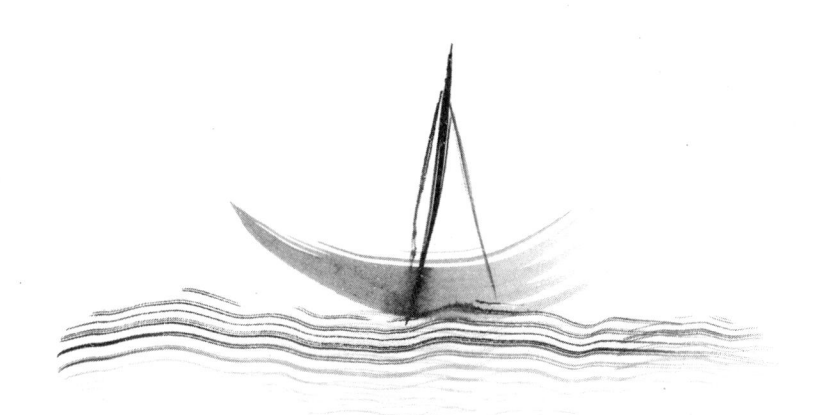

*Rushing waves
listen,
– a sudden silence*

*Distant drums,*
*ocean of clouds*
*my quivering arrow*
*searching*
*the unseen target*

*This fleeting cloud,*
*let me stitch it*
*on to my quilt*

*My offering
to the wind gods
— a line sketched
across the sky*

*Autumn forest
dream
upon dream,
falling*

*Flowers gathered
through many springs
— scattered like
autumn leaves*

*Dusk*
*a lone hibiscus*
*burning with fire*
*— the scarlet sea*

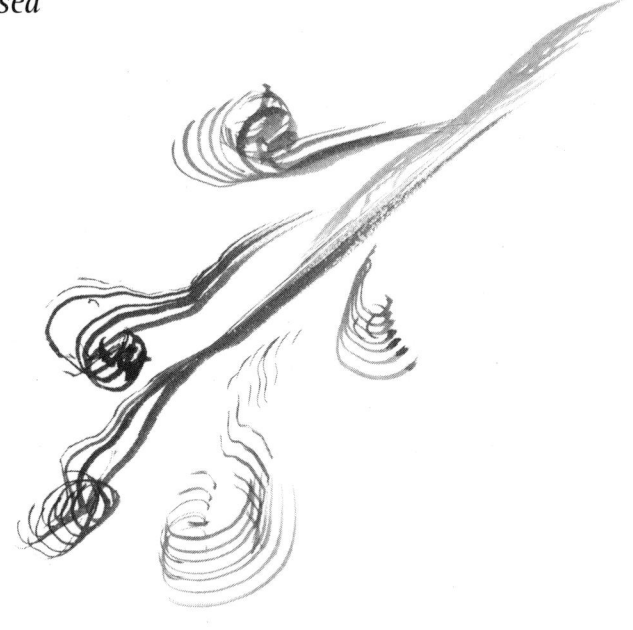

*Shadow of
warm pebbles,
a snail
– hiding*

*The white summit
saffron robes flying
— an eagle's cry*

*Prayer wheels spinning
silence in Buddha's eyes
— murmuring heartbeats*

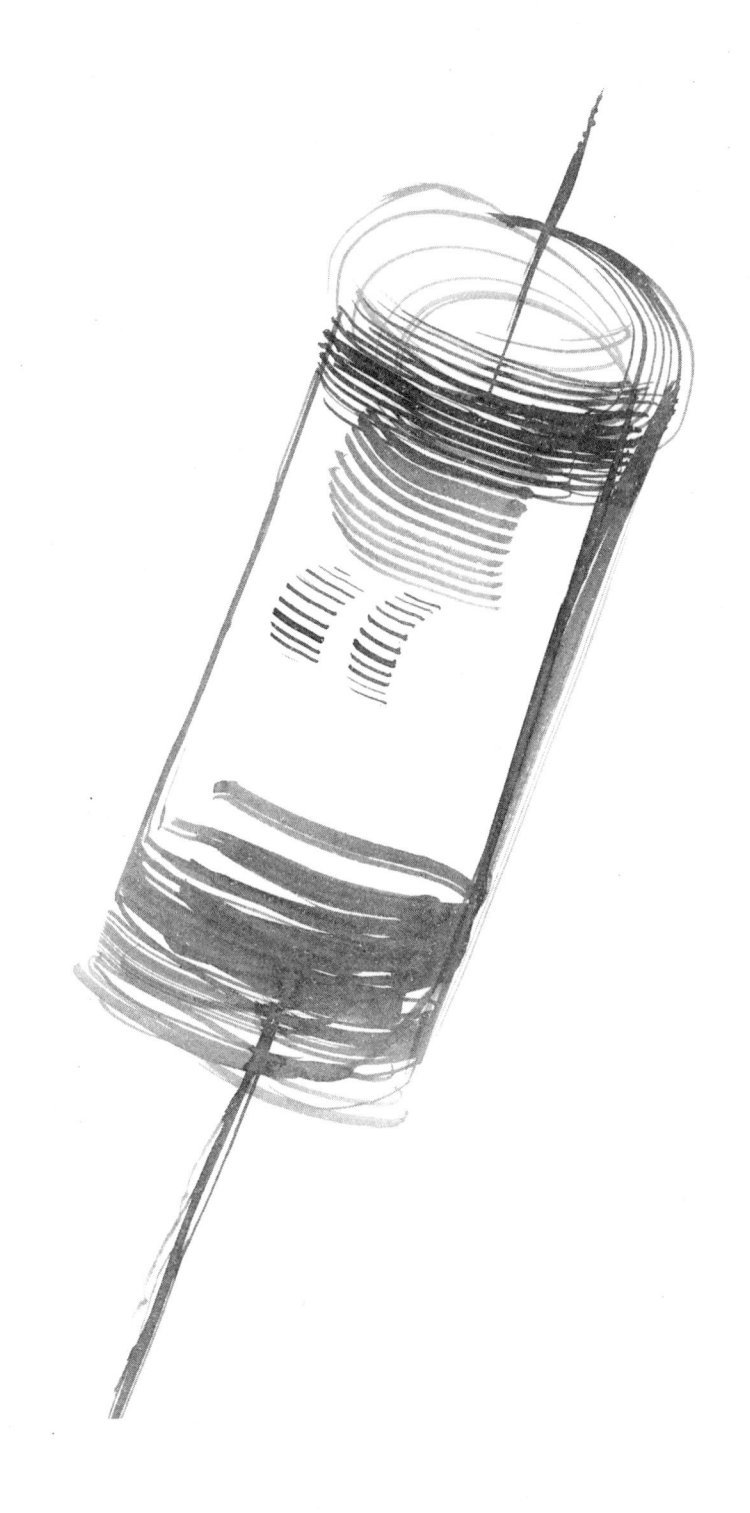

*A tear in
Buddha's eye
– dry the boundless ocean*

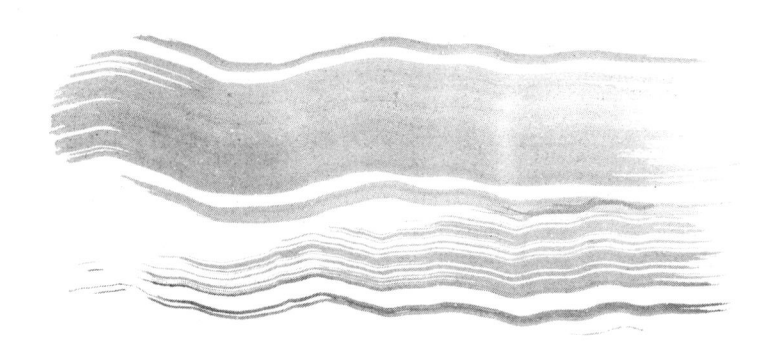

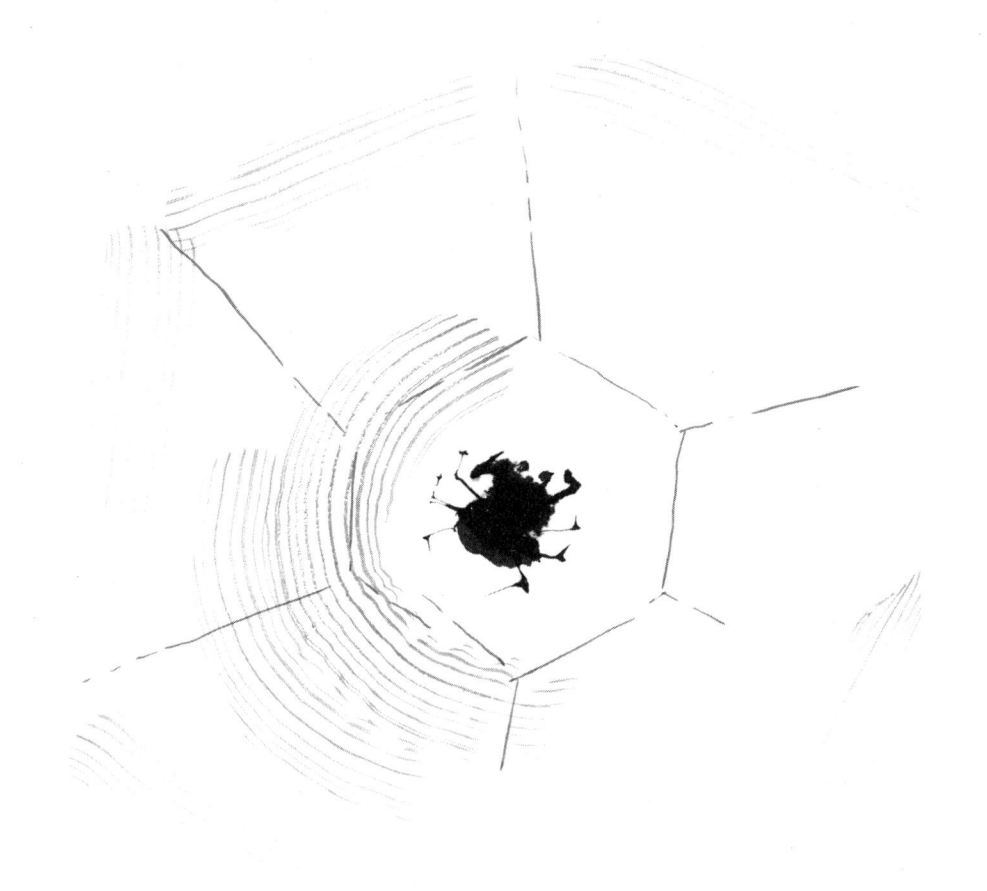

*Don't stop spider
– the world may
stop spinning*

# Still Waters

*Incidents and Anecdotes*

# Ascent

The rich nobleman had just returned after a very successful venture from the neighbouring province. He had made a great profit and felt that it would be a good idea to make a small offering at the monastery on the snow-clad summit.

Effortlessly he climbed the thousand steps to the beautiful monastery hidden behind the clouds. He met the wise roshi, and said his prayers. He made an offering and relieved his conscience. After all, he had used some unfair means to achieve his goals! The next step up the ladder to fame and riches was to meet the emperor, after which he would be in a commanding position. The nobleman felt good after meeting the roshi. He became reassured that there would be no further obstacles in his meteoric rise.

The roshi said, 'Why don't you come with me to the valley? I have to give sermons there.' They started walking down the steps.

'Master, please slow down, my knee hurts! It is very painful going down the steps. I wonder why? Going up was no problem.'

The master slowed to let the rich man catch his breath. He smiled and put his reassuring hand on the nobleman's shoulder and said, 'When you will become as comfortable going downhill as you are going uphill, then you will have arrived somewhere. Bear the pain and find your balance, because life goes up and down; constantly.'

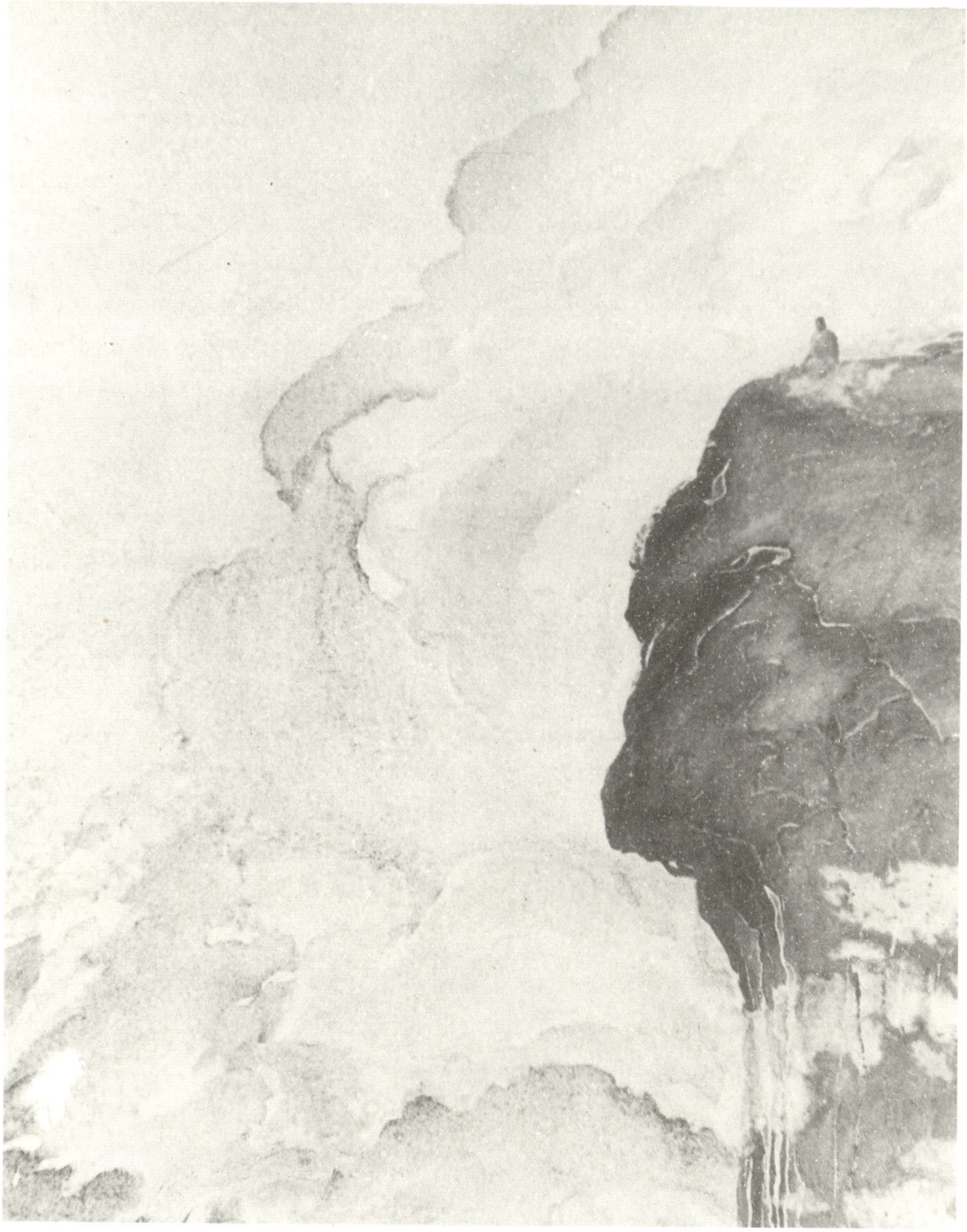

# Possession

Said the Zen Master to his disciples, 'We lose sleep, suffer pain, become jealous, angry and frustrated by the desire to possess: be it a beautiful person, or an object.

'Beauty, love, or a precious person can never be possessed. Can we really possess a wild flower? One may own the petals, the stem and the pollen; one may even bottle the fragrance. But the moment one tries to hold it still or lock it in, the beauty dissipates. The flower is no more.

'The only way one can possess is to be one with the spirit, its essence. Then one becomes the object of one's desire – there is no conflict, gain or loss. It is a continuous flow.

'The infinite is where ultimate beauty resides.'

The Zen Master continued speaking to his disciples. 'There was once a handsome and ornate mirror. People were so attracted to it, that they all wanted to possess it.

'It passed through many hands. Many wise men, kings and emperors owned it. Many beautiful women possessed it too.

'The essential property of a mirror is its ability to reflect. Like our minds, its essence is to remain crystal clear - to give back what it receives. Not to own. The trouble was that this mirror wanted to possess its owners too.

'It was very proud to be so cherished. Each time someone looked at the image in it, the mirror captured the image forever.

'Over time the mirror became cloudy with overlapping images. Granted, they were majestic images, but the mirror continued to fog till there was just a little spot of its own reflective self in the centre.

'One day there was a radiant sunrise, ethereal and beautiful. The mirror fell in love with it and tried its best to retain the image. However, the image was too radiant, the heat too strong for the reflective spot on the mirror to hold.

'The mirror shattered into tiny fragments – cold as granite.'

# Deceit

The dzong, a fortress-monastery, had stood rooted at the confluence of two mighty rivers almost since time began. A few hundred yards away stood a tiny island with a small chorten on it. This was a stone structure, a few feet high, dedicated to Buddha. It was believed that if ever anything were to happen to this little chorten – the monumental dzong would fall, and with it would fall Dharma.

For centuries, people used to come and worship at the little chorten. Slowly it became imbued with mysterious and magical qualities. It had to withstand many floods, lightning and earthquakes. Located on a very strong rock, it also had to withstand the force of the river's current, which swept past the little island.

Once, over ten days and ten nights, it rained incessantly. The eleventh night was terrifying. There was thunder and lightning, such as never seen before. Even the first few floors of the dzong were flooded.

There was panic. The earth shook with a deafening noise, and the small chorten, the holiest magical chorten collapsed!

The Zen master witnessed this collapse. Instantly he summoned his strongest disciple and said, 'Go quickly and rebuild the chorten immediately.'

The mighty monk flexed his muscles, took a deep breath and fought the torrential waters of the two great rivers. Stone by stone, through the dark night, he rebuilt the chorten till it looked exactly as before.

At last it was daybreak. The waters subsided. It was peaceful and calm.

A great throng of people had assembled at the confluence marvelling at the magical powers of the chorten. They praised it for having saved the dzong and their lives. Their faith in Buddha grew even more. They went back reassured and fearless, ready to fight the effects of the flood.

The disciple said, 'But master, that was deceitful, how could you make me a part of your lie? Is this your religion? Is this how the great Buddha functions?'

The Master replied: 'No, but sometimes people need to believe in miracles...which is why I made you rebuild the chorten. Seeing it standing helped to overcome fear and panic. In that moment of crisis, they were able to fight the flood and summon the strength to save countless lives.'

'The power of Buddha is beyond it all...he does not need to show his strength by saving the chorten or the dzong. Why...the river itself is Buddha. Rivers must flow, and from time to time, also overflow. Floods represent renewal. In the aftermath they bring the riches of the earth to the surface for sentient beings. They make the soil fertile. They renew life. That is why the Buddha made the river sweep everything in its path.'

'Sooner or later people will realize what actually happened. By that time they would have already gone past the critical period. They will know the truth – for in the dark of night you have rebuilt the chorten backwards!'

# Nomad

After days of wandering through the desolate mountains, the sunburnt roshi paused and said to the monks, 'We are all born, essentially, as nomads. Yes, we need a mother's warm embrace and a father's reassuring presence, but our spirit is free. We are not born rooted or in chains. In fact we even break out of the womb - the most secure place.'

'The natural process is to unfetter ourselves and experience the freedom of insecurity. Soon our fears and conditioning bring us right back to the prison. From being carefree nomads we become rooted like milestones, making our prison more and more comfortable, secure and glamorous till the self delusion is complete, and we forget that we are in a jail. We defend it with all our might.'

'We all seek security, but are we ever secure? A beggar may feel secure once he has amassed a thousand coins and has a tin shed over his head, but soon he will want more and there begins another circle of insecurity.'

'Even nations are not free from this web of insecurity. They may conquer neighbouring countries and build an empire. But even with the empire at hand, the fear of losing it will propel them to create defences and horrible weapons to crush and destroy their enemies - all in the name of security.'

'However, somewhere, deep down, the nomad in us refuses to be chained. Sometimes we break out of the jail by immersing ourselves into ephemeral moments that allow us a glimpse of the infinite. A beautiful sunrise, the reflection of the moon on lapping waves, or a whiff of a fragrance that evokes lost childhood: these moments are very precious as they allow us to touch the nomad within us. We become vast like the ocean.

The trick is to return to being the fearless nomad, who is secure wherever he is.'

'Between the tired fires of dusk and the newborn fires of dawn, between the flapping of your wings and your flight, between the boat sailing and sinking, between sleep and wakefulness, between the flower and the fruit, is where true security is. In the ever-changing, yet changeless, is the real home.'

# Sharing

There was a nomad who, separated from his caravan, travelled alone on vast sands for a long time. One day his camel too collapsed. Still, the nomad went on. For days on end, in the blistering heat, without food or water, he slumped and crawled, ready to exhaust his last breath. Till, at last, he saw a lone palm tree.

Was it a mirage or real? He did not care. His only hope was for some water near the tree and shade under which he could rest and recuperate. Renewed with this hope, he made a tremendous effort to reach the shelter.

The tree watched all this, but was unwilling to give of himself to this intruder. It shouted, 'Get out of my sight. I do not want to share my shadow with you. How dare you steal my precious shadow?' The nomad, bleary-eyed with exhaustion and deprivation, looked up at the scrawny tree and replied: 'I am sorry for intruding sir, but perhaps you do not realize that it is noon. You have no shadow to give me even if you wished to.'

# Aesthete

In a remote village at the base of an ethereal mountain there lived a young artist.

He was privileged to have studied the art of calligraphy from the old Zen master at the Blue Dragon monastery. He had a deep insight into the workings of a great mind. From him he learned the power of a simple dynamic stroke, the value of empty space, the balance of asymmetry. Slowly, he refined his eye to such a degree that if at the tea ceremony there was a millimetre moe of space than was needed between the bowl and the tea whisk, it made him terribly uncomfortable.

The master would lay these traps for him on purpose, sometimes making the stem of the peony a bit too tall for the vase it was arranged in, or placing his tatami mat slightly askew or not cleaning the used butter lamp before lighting it again. He would watch the artist to see if he had noticed and would smile reassuringly when the artist would gracefully set them right.

He used to frequent local antique shops in search of tea ceremony bowls for his master. One particular shop with its blue tiled roof specialized in objects crafted out of jade. He especially admired an intricately carved jade dagger which was always kept locked in a glass case as it was deemed the most precious object in the shop. Around it were rare scrolls by Seshu and other Zen masters. He thought that someday he too would be able to paint with the same force.

After studying and copying the works of great masters for a long time, he finally developed his own style. Soon, he had a great reputation and his work was much admired and sought after. And many people wanted to visit his studio.

One of these was a beautiful young woman, the daughter of a nobleman. She would often come to the studio and spend a lot of time there, though she looked more at the artist than at his creations. She admired his hands with which he created such powerful works. She adored his understated kimono, with its grey and deep charcoal grey pattern. She loved the way he moved with catlike grace to show her a new scroll he had just painted. He, in turn was mesmerized by her languid eyes, her spontaneous laughter, and the mysterious aura surrounding her.

It was only natural that they fell in love.

They spent a lot of time together, sharing many seasons, observing different moons. It was perfect, an ideal state. But soon the girl's parents grew concerned about her future and wondered when the artist was going to propose to her. They waited patiently and so did the girl, but one day her patience ran out, also she was concerned about her parents' deteriorating health. So the young woman took it upon herself to ask the artist to marry her.

The artist would not hear of it. The perfectionist in him could not imagine marriage with all its mundane problems. He wanted to paint quietly with nothing to disturb his pristine world. So he refused to get married.

The doe-eyed beauty left him alone and went back home. She just looked at him one last time at the doorway and disappeared into the night.

The artist was stunned. He could not imagine life without her. And so, at the crack of dawn he sent her a flaming hibiscus, fresh with dew and a scroll of the misty mountain she admired and asked her to come back to him.

She did.

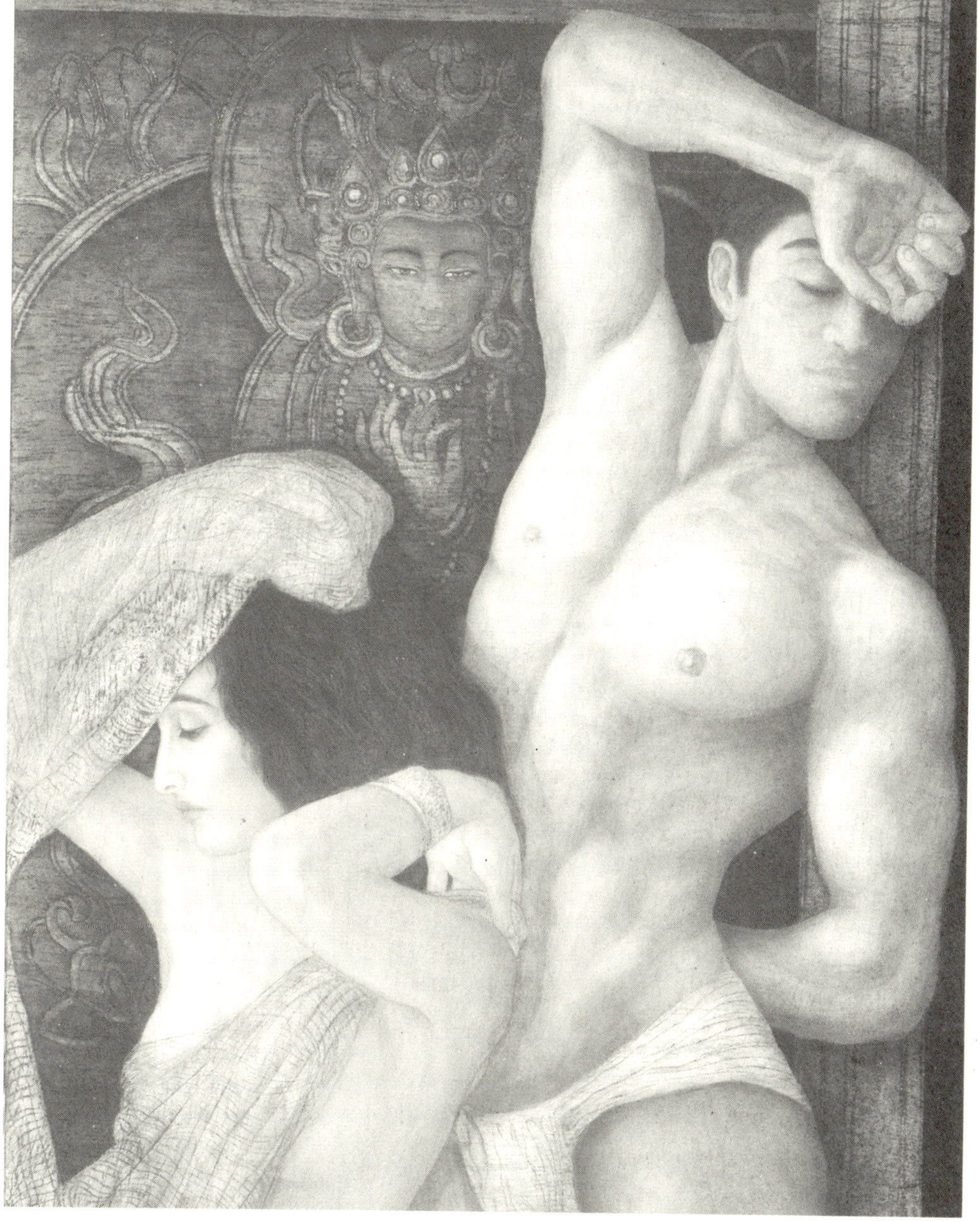

Soon it was as before, an ideal state. But when she repeated the question, she received the same answer. She would leave. He would repent and beg her to come back, repeating the ritual.

Distressed, she bade him a final goodbye.

Months went by, the artist waited, sure that she would reappear. He could not paint, could not draw. All he thought of was her beautiful eyes.

He did not try to contact her, loving her too much to put her through the same torture again – yet unsure of coping with the imperfection of marriage that could destroy his perfectly aesthetic world.

This dilemma was driving him insane. The only way out was to take his life.

He thought of taking poison, but it seemed too cowardly. He thought of hanging himself, but his senses reeled at the ugly image that filled his mind. Jumping off the cliff? No! That would spoil the purity of the white snow below!

And then it struck him – the jade dagger was the answer, the perfect way to go. He could not think of a more beautiful way to die.

He had to have the dagger and so he hurried to the antique shop.

The artist asked the greedy shopkeeper the price and was astonished at his answer.

He couldn't possibly afford it. Seeing the melancholic look on his face, and knowing the value of his works, the shopkeeper made him an offer – he could pay for the dagger with his scrolls.

Delighted, the artist brought him all the scrolls he had painted over the years and which were still with him. 'Not enough, not enough! Bring some more,' said the shopkeeper.

The artist is now fifty-two years old. He works furiously and from time to time he carries his scrolls to the shop hoping one day to be able to complete his payment and finally own the exquisite jade dagger.

Meanwhile, his scrolls have become outstanding.

Occasionally the shopkeeper pulls out the key from his secret cabinet and lets the trembling hands of the artist caress the jade dagger, his salvation.

# Secret

The samurai lord, commanding in an intricately chased silver armour, took a deep breath, battle fatigued after looting and plundering the fifth Emperor.

He instructed his men to load all the loot on to the saddles of his horses while he rested.

Ready to start at dawn on his next voyage, the samurai lord set out to strike terror in the hearts of men in the next village.

The village was very poor; there was nothing for his army to plunder. Frustrated, he asked his hostages where the wealth lay. Where hid the rich?

He kept hearing the same answer, 'there are no riches in this village.' And yet the villagers seemed happy and content.

The samurai started beating and torturing the hostages till one of them broke down, saying, 'the old roshi at the monastery ... he has the ultimate wealth. He is the richest in the land. He has the rare Buddha's cylinder – it has been handed over from generation to generation - which lets him view paradise. Why...his sermons of his visions of paradise are what keeps us happy and content. Once a year, when the moon is full, he lets us peer through the cylinder and we are blissful' The cunning samurai thought that if the villagers can be so happy just by looking though the cylinder once a year, surely if he possessed it and saw paradise, he could break the gates open and all the wealth of paradise would be his. Releasing the hostages and asking for directions to the monastery, he galloped off in a hurry, without waiting even for his army.

He expected the monastery to have at least a gilded Buddha statue but there was nothing. A dark empty room was all that was there.

Moonlight filtered in through a little window in the wall behind the roshi, who was meditating.

Breaking the calm, the samurai held his sword at the neck of the roshi and thundered, 'I know you have the precious Buddha's cylinder...Hand it to me or else I will slit your throat.'

Unperturbed, the roshi simply smiled, even as the cold metal of the blade pressed deeper into his neck.

The room was bare. There was nothing in the room except an incense holder and a scroll on the wall with an image of Buddha.

Irritated by the roshi's smile and fearlessness, the samurai pushed him down on the wooden floor. There, to his delight, he saw a few loose planks where the roshi had been sitting.

He pried the planks apart, and in a little cavity in the floor he found what he was looking for.

Carefully wrapped in layers of silk was the treasure: Buddha's cylinder.

The samurai's fingers trembled as he opened the packet. He gingerly handled the cylinder, a strange contraption. On the large end of the plain metal cylinder was mounted a piece of polished round glass. On the other end, as he pulled, smaller and smaller pieces of tubes kept extending out till at the small end was another piece of glass, just wide enough for an eye.

Quickly he figured it out. This then was the ultimate treasure, which would let him see the gates of Paradise, ready to be plundered.

The samurai pointed the cylinder through the window. But all he could see was the valley below. Yes, in greater detail. He could even see the bell on the ox as the little boy took him grazing. But where were the gates of paradise? He pointed it in different directions but to no avail.

Then he realized that it was not night yet and the full moon was still a long way off.

He waited day after day, night after night for the full moon.

He saw the roshi meditating, reciting the Lotus Sutra endlessly with a beautiful smile on his lips.

Having nothing better to do, the Samurai also sat cross-legged, thinking that perhaps the secret of viewing paradise lay in some trick in the posture of the roshi.

He sat in this posture night after night but was still unable to figure out any trick that the roshi might know.

He thought, perhaps it was in the chanting of the mantra before the full moon that the trick lay. He started chanting too. But still the secret eluded him.

Oh! The roshi does not eat or drink while I keep eating the delicious food of dried fish and nuts, the delectable sweets that I stole from the fifth Emperor.

He gave up food too, thinking that the trick lay in starving. But still the samurai could not figure out the secret.

Maybe, it is the way the roshi breathes...the way he takes these long breaths and releases them as he chants. The Samurai sat cross-legged, recited the sutra and breathed like the roshi, starving and waiting for the moon to become full.

It was time...a full year has passed. There was just one night left for the full moon. By this time meditation had become second nature to the Samurai.

He thought of all the people he had killed, all the cities he had plundered, all the women he had left widowed, crying with their children, the crops he had burnt for fun, the rubies around his neck, the gold and emerald bracelet of the Emperor whose hands he had chopped off and whom he had beheaded.

These things no longer gave him any pleasure. He was becoming happier just sitting and chanting, even though his legs were aching, his back painfully erect and his stomach rumbling from hunger.

And yet, the desire for the riches of Paradise still lingered.

At last it was the night of the full moon.

He took Buddha's cylinder out of the silk wrapping, rushed to the window and pointed the cylinder to the moon, extending the tube out, putting his eye to the smaller end, ready to view magnificent Paradise. He saw the glowing orb, with its silver light, but no gates, no gates to Paradise.

Panic-stricken, he called out to the roshi, 'Tell me if it is true, surely it must be true that Buddha's cylinder lets you see Paradise. Why else would you hide this object if it were worthless? What is the secret? What is the trick?'

'Of course it is true...Buddha's cylinder does not deceive,' said the roshi.

'Only in your hurry to take the cylinder you forgot to take the essential second part. Here it is. You may have it.'

The samurai snatched the small packet from the roshi's hands and tore apart the silk wrapping. Inside was a small flat and round piece of metal with two hooks at the sides. They fitted perfectly on the large, round glass of the cylinder, matching the holes on the tube.

There was utter darkness. The glowing moon reflected in the cylinder became dark. Slowly, the samurai sank to his knees and sat cross-legged again.

The roshi was chanting mantras and he smiled at the samurai.

The samurai understood: the cap that darkened the view from Buddha's cylinder had made him give up looking for the gates to Paradise.

With his superficial view of life blocked, the transformed Samurai discovered the glowing paradise within himself.

The long time that he had spent in meditating had not been wasted.

He smiled back at the roshi, sharing his secret.

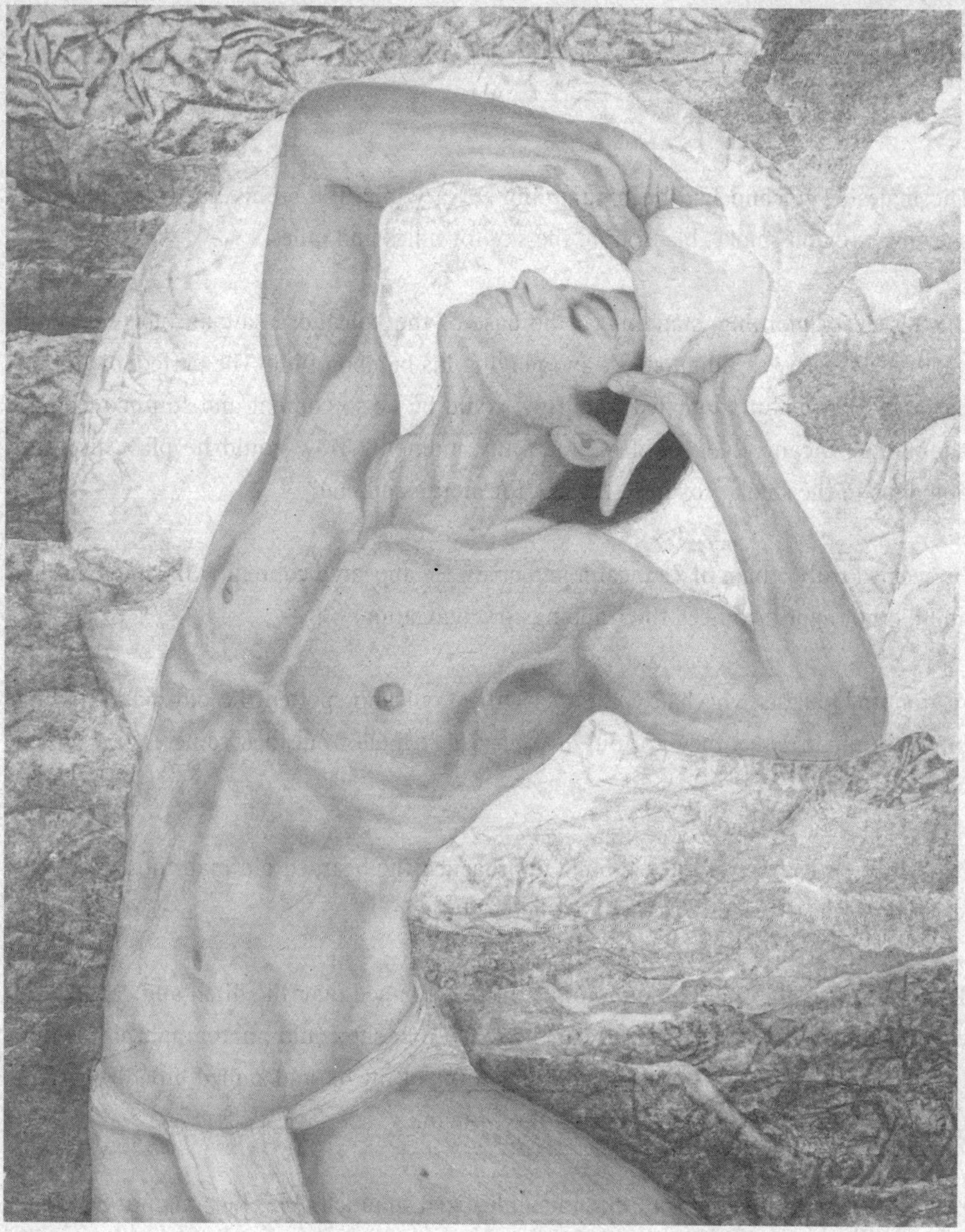

# Appearance

The majestic volcano had been rumbling for a while. It was hissing like a dragon, spewing fire and smoke, blackening the sky for miles and miles.

On this misty morning, standing at the base of the volcano, I saw an old man amid paddy fields. He was riding an ox and playing his bamboo flute. The perfect picture of harmony with nature, I envied him. How could he be so content and so unconcerned about the volcano that could explode any moment? How could he play his flute oblivious to the smoke covering the sky for months on end?

He seemed truly a man of Zen, calm in a crisis. He appeared content with simple things and did not appear to need the trappings of civilization.

A group of tourists who had come to visit the volcano spotted the old man. Finding him very picturesque, they got out of their vehicle, pulled out their cameras and started clicking.

An attractive woman of a large build approached the bearded old man to get a closer shot but stopped abruptly at the ditch between them.

To my surprise, the frail old man got off his ox, jumped over the ditch and carried the woman across. He put her down near the ox so that she could photograph him better. He knelt down, raised his arms to hold the horns of the ox and smiled broadly, certain that he would receive a large tip from the woman.

I was horrified. Is this the man that I had idealized so much? Was he a man of Zen, one

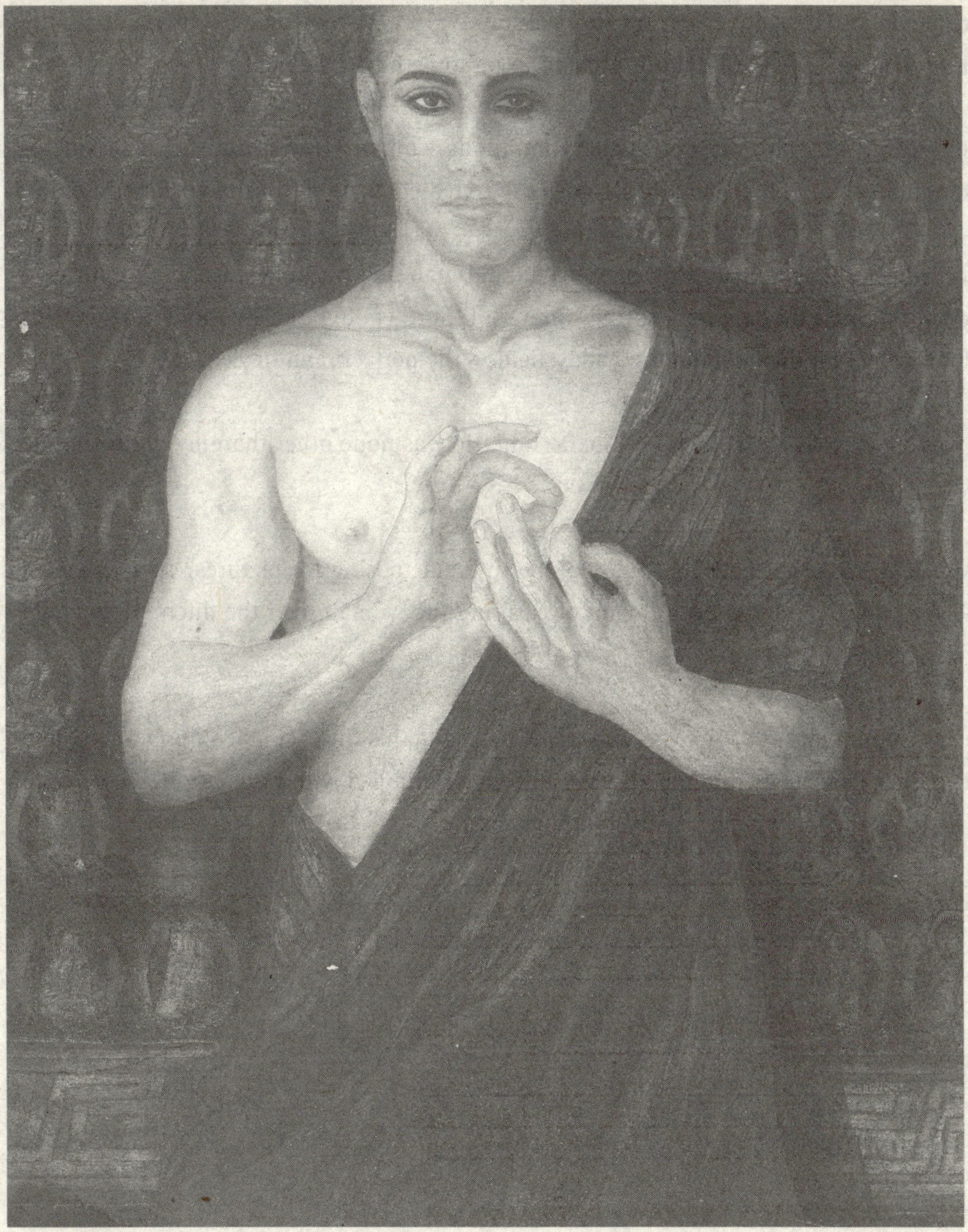

with nature? The idol fell from its pedestal. No, I was much better off with all my shortcomings. At least I did not pretend to be something I was not.

How could this old man touch the voluptuous woman? How could he abandon his tranquillity for a bit of money? Disgusted, I retreated, waiting for the volcano to erupt.

My mind could not rest. It dwelled on the old man and his antics. Unable to put it to rest, I returned the next day to the same spot. Sure enough, he was there playing his flute, seated on the ox amid the paddy fields - the perfect man of Zen.

I was shocked as I took a closer look at him. He was none other than my old roshi, the wise monk.

Appalled, I asked him, 'How could you be so crude, posing for pictures? I am ashamed of you. How could you even dream of carrying the woman over the ditch? How could you accept money?'

'It paid for my bowl of rice,' he said, as he picked up his flute, climbed upon the ox and merrily ambled away into the distance. His music mingled with smoke from the volcano and filled the misty valley with soothing calm.

A perfect man of Zen!

# Silence

Galloping horses, a roaring sea and a thundering sky – they can all be silent. It all depends on our perception, a particular frame of mind, at a particular time.

Some moons ago, I was desperately trying to meditate in a very noisy room in a monastery. The monks were repairing the old building and replacing rotting, wooden beams, constantly hammering, talking in loud voices. Mosquitoes buzzed above my ears. I waited for night to descend so that the noise would settle and I could have peace and quiet.

My aged roshi had caught a chill and had a coughing bout. He coughed incessantly. Try as he might, he just could not stop coughing. His coughing, mixed with other sounds, continued for days and nights. It was enough to drive me out of my mind. I longed for a bit of silence, some tranquillity. Unable to go out of the room and leave my beloved roshi alone, I prayed that somehow the sound of his coughing should stop. There should be silence...there must be silence...I had to have my silence.

A few nights later, as I stepped out of the room for a few moments to gaze at the new moon, I heard a loud scream from the young monk who had brought Miso soup for the roshi.

There was silence.

The revered roshi had suffered a stroke and his voice had gone. He could not cough, nor cry for help. He could not even say where it hurt, or what he wanted. All the monks became depressed. A pall of gloom hung over the monastery. The work on the new building ceased. Everybody became silent and prayed quietly.

There was the silence I had longed for...yet, I could not meditate.

Days went by. We lost all hope of his voice returning. There were tears in his eyes; tears of sorrow, of pain and anguish over the unfinished monastery. Following a long and silent night spent alone with him, as the first rays of the sun struck his face through the window, he held my hand and, almost inaudibly, whispered my name. Again and again ... almost like a mantra.

I yearned for all the sounds, and his voice, to return.

Even the sound of his coughing would have been welcome.

# Prison

A young and enterprising businessman, who was dissatisfied with life, went to a monk to seek advice. The monk took him to a tearoom to relax and offered him a cup of tea.

'Often, I feel that life has not given me enough. Why does my neighbour have more than me? Don't I deserve more, if not the same? What is so special about him? I am more intelligent and I work twice as hard. I am honest, I pray regularly and I even take good care of my ailing grandmother. Isn't it unfair? Why are things so difficult for me and so easy for him?'

Sipping his tea, the monk nodded his head and pointed to the Zen garden outside the tearoom. Viewed from a small low window, the garden, made of a grouping of just seven rocks, some large, some small and fine gravel raked around them, appeared very small.

'What you are saying is so true. I also felt the same way when we were constructing this garden. Why did we not have a much bigger space in our monastery for the garden? The garden next door is so big compared to ours. What is more, the monks next door did not even have to work for it. They just inherited it, while we were building the rock garden for months. We carted these heavy rocks on our backs all the way from the distant mountain. We sweated through a very hot summer and shivered through winter with the cold winds chilling our bones. The monks next door had an easy life getting up at dawn, while we were up at three a.m., chanting the sutras and digging holes for the huge rocks so that they could be embedded in the earth.

'We were tired and frustrated and envious of the garden next door. One day I dared to ask our roshi the same question, "Why is our garden so small, don't we deserve a bigger one?"'

'The roshi did not say anything but walked to the grouping of rocks, realigned them slightly to repeat the profile of the mountain in the distance, the top of which we could just about see behind the tall stone wall enclosing the garden.'

The roshi said, 'You are right. The garden is too small. Why don't we do something about it? Surely we don't deserve such a small garden.' Saying this he picked up a hammer, walked to the wall made of stone and started knocking it down. I was shocked when he asked all the monks to do the same, to join him in knocking down our security.

'We kept hammering till just a remnant of the wall was left, barely defining the compound.'

Having finishing drinking the tea, the monk led the businessman outside the tearoom.

'Yes, our garden was too small, but don't you think that by removing the wall, the distant mountain with all its magnificence has become part of our garden? Hasn't the space become vast? Now there is no difference between our neighbour's garden and ours. In fact, ours is almost infinite.'

'To be happy, we needed to become vast and part of a larger universe. All we had to do was to remove the imprisoning wall.'

'Do the same with your mental prison, you too will become content.'

# Habit

There was a small industrial town on the way to a mountain resort. People passing through this town had to cover their noses with a cloth, so overpowering was the stench of the fumes from the chemical plant. Tourists dreaded having to go through this town but the inhabitants were oblivious. They could not care less and went about their business as if the foul smell did not exist.

One day an environmentalist was passing through the town and was appalled by the situation.

He approached the commissioner of the town and asked him how he could help.

'What are you talking about?' the commissioner asked.

'The foul smell of course...it's bad for health.'

'Oh that! It's no problem at all. Only when there is a very strong easterly wind do we feel something, but that happens very rarely. What we need in this town is a good cinema... don't you know somebody who wants to invest? He could earn millions. I have this large piece of land where he could build...you can have your cut if you can find someone rich, we could all make a bit of money...'

The environmentalist was horrified, but he had a plan and wanted to enlighten the commissioner so that he could do some good for the polluted town. Without revealing his true intentions he said, 'That's a good idea...yes, I know just the person who lives in the mountains next to the place I am building...and yes, the extra money would come in handy to finish building my home. Why don't you come with me and I will introduce you to him.'

The commissioner went along with the environmentalist, who heaved a sigh of relief, having at last left the town.

The drive up the mountains was blissful, with clean fresh air and the White Mountains were already visible. In the distance he could see the monastery with the fluttering prayer flags, where he often worshipped.

Soon they were close to the idyllic place. Cool fresh air wafted through the car. The environmentalist noticed that as they went up the mountains, the commissioner started breathing heavily.

'You are looking unwell, why don't we stop at the monastery and have a cup of green tea. I know the monks here and they won't mind. Besides the fresh air will do you good.'

The monk at the monastery served them tea while they sat on a wooden bench under the magnolia tree. The pristine peaks glistened with the glow of the setting sun.

The environmentalist noticed that the commissioner was feeling more and more ill. Thinking that he would revive and truly appreciate the value of a clear environment, the environmentalist gently picked up a fragrant Magnolia flower and offered it to the commissioner to inhale.

The commissioner reluctantly brought it close to his nose and shouted, 'Is this a joke? The whole sermon about fresh air, it makes me sick. And God, how this flower stinks... Take me back to my home now!'

# Winning and Losing

There was a billionaire who spent his life amassing wealth. His fortune was made when very young. On his property there was a labourer his age. The labourer had toiled and toiled for a long time, yet was unable to make two ends meet.

One day the labourer lost his job. He had no one to turn to. In desperation he gambled the last bit of his money on a lottery ticket hoping his fortune would turn. The billionaire invested a lot of money in a new venture certain of multiplying his wealth ten fold.

The market crashed and the billionaire lost 50 million.

Meanwhile, it so happened that the super bumper lottery ticket that the labourer had bought also worth 50 million.

By a twist of fate the labourer won the lottery at the same time as the billionaire lost his money on the new venture.

The moment they heard the news, they both suffered a heart attack. One died out of joy, the other out of sorrow!

Both won. Both lost.

# Nothingness

'It was terrible, master. Our whole world has come to an end... the barbarians, the barbarians! I cannot forget their sinister smiles as they hit and smashed. The glee with which they went about hitting our Buddha, the wise one who has stood there for centuries, guiding us with his message of peace. Oh! The barbarians, they shrieked with joy, each time a piece of the sacred Buddha fell to the ground. I could not bear it any longer, master. I stood there frozen with anger and fright. I tried to capture those stones with my robes as they fell, master. It was horrible. The earth itself trembled as the barbarians went about in a mad frenzy.'

'The Buddha stood there for a long time, stoic, with a magnificent smile on his face. But alas, he fell. Shelled and stoned, completely mutilated, he crumbled to the ground, powdered into nothingness!'

The roshi put his arm around the sobbing monk and said with a smile, 'Why do you despair? Isn't nothingness what Buddha is all about?'

# Rebellion

The young rebellious acolyte was unable to sit cross-legged any longer in the lotus posture while chanting the mantras with other monks in the three-hour long session before daybreak. He found the chanting boring and monotonous. During the session they were not allowed to talk or whisper, or glance sideways. The regimen was well defined: Arise at four am, then, a cold bath, an hour of exercise and a recitation of the sutras. After a modest breakfast, they had to clean up the monastery. This was followed by another session of meditation, after which the roshi answered their philosophical queries. A short rest, then training in the martial arts followed by more meditation till dinnertime, when they ate some vegetables and boiled rice.

The young monk's legs ached, his back hurt and his mind wandered. The sound of chanting was getting on his nerves. Through the corner of his eye he watched a cat peeping in from the shoji window. The young monk leapt up and chased the cat out of the window.

There was a hushed silence. The monks were shocked. This was taboo. One never ever disturbed the chanting. They looked apprehensively at the roshi and wondered what kind of punishment the young monk would receive.

The roshi asked the monk to come to the jade room.

There he said, 'Yes, I understand that you do not want to follow the rules. It is natural for the young to be rebellious. After all, why should you follow the path laid down by our ancestors? They also stumbled, struggled groped for answers till they found what was right for them. Go ahead. Break the rules...find out what is right for you. Just remember one thing: you have to be conscious of what the limitations are. How can you get out of a prison without being aware of its boundaries?'

The acolyte was stunned at the master's words and a bit ashamed of himself. He said, 'Roshi, I find the endless sessions of chanting the mantras boring. The spartan life is pointless, the frugal food is miserable. Even though I am committed to monkhood and want to discover the truth, be one with the Buddha, I find all the rules and regulations superfluous. Can I not do things my way without hurting others?'

'That is impossible,' said the roshi, adding, 'you will hurt others if you don't follow the path. Do not be afraid of this. Maybe it will jolt the others into being conscious of the chosen path, for one should not follow the way without understanding its essence. If your colleagues are blindly chanting the mantras or turning the prayer wheel mechanically, it is of no use. If they are serving the poor without any passion in their compassion it is worthless. If they ring the prayer bell without listening to its pure sound, it is a crime.

'Have the courage of your convictions. It is a lonely path I assure you. It has its own responsibilities. Tough as it may seem, it has its own rewards. Sooner or later you will realize that you cannot rebel forever. You cannot live in a state of chaos infinitely. Your very rebellion will form a pattern which will transform into a grid. Different it may be, but it will still be a grid. Whether the grid is a prison to be broken or an armature to strengthen your spirit is the question.

'The Tao is about natural order. There is infinite beauty to be found if you live in harmony with it.'

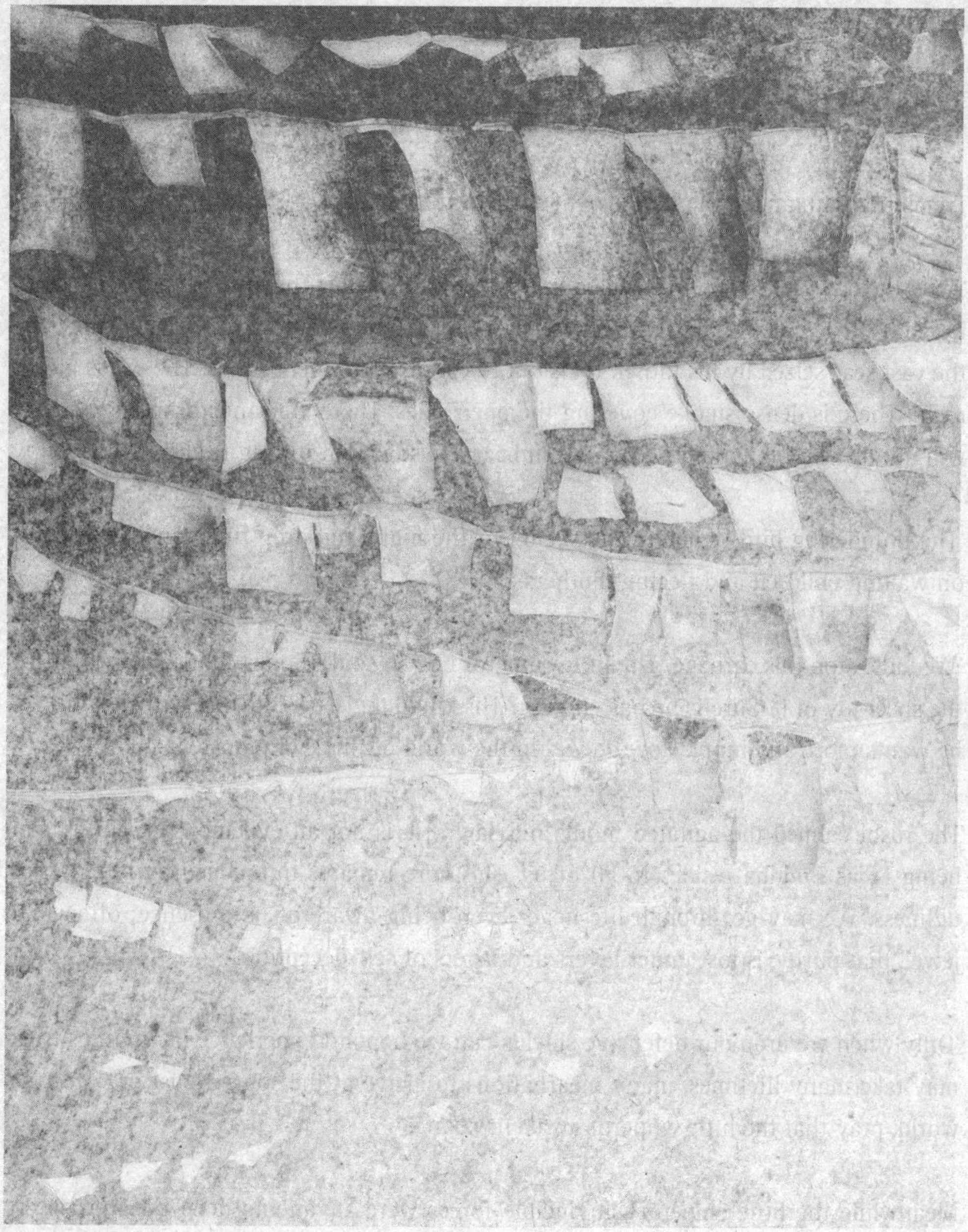

# The Jewel

Trembling with anger, the Monk went rushing to the Roshi.

'After the havoc the emperor created in this land of Buddha, the little emperor has done it again. He is not content with the snow-clad mountains and the verdant valleys or the vast seas seized by his father. He is out to conquer the silent sands. The sands bleed, roshi. There is dense smoke covering the open skies. There are sandstorms raging that will not die for a long, long time. The unbearable stench of rotting flesh is everywhere.

'The thundering birds come in the shelter of the night and drop fire from their bellies on wailing children and fleeing mothers.

'We must stop this carnage. The little emperor has no soul. He just kills for greed or for the sheer joy of it. Surely, he has enough? His kingdom is overflowing with wealth, yet he wants more and more. How do we rid the world of this evil monster?'

The roshi calmed the agitated monk and said, 'He is not an evil monster. No human being is, as Buddha resides in all of us. This core remains untouched by all exterior ugliness. We may go through life never even being aware of its presence; often that jewel, that purity, is lost under layers and layers of self-deception.

'Only when we drop our defensive shields can we hope to experience its luminosity. It may take many lifetimes, many incarnations to arrive at the source. Just pray for the world, pray that the little emperor awakens soon.'

Meanwhile the little emperor's invincible forces were advancing deep into the desert kingdom; there was pain and immense suffering wherever they went. To plan future strategy, the little emperor summoned a council of his most trusted aides and sycophants who kept pushing him to further ruthlessness.

He did not sleep for days and nights. So occupied was he with planning the war, gloating over his successes, that he had no time for his beloved dog.

The beautiful dog, so used to love being showered on him, was totally ignored. The dog was totally himself, one with his inner and outer self. It did not matter to him whether he was the pet of an emperor or a pauper. He was the only one in the whole kingdom who could jump on the little emperor's lap, lick his arrogant face while in deep sleep, or demand food at unearthly hours by simply wagging his tail. The dog was blissful all the time. All he wanted was affection. Food when hungry, a walk when in need of exercise and sleep when tired: a true Zen being.

Suddenly bad news came in from the desert. The little emperor's plan had failed. He left the war council in a huff, not wanting to confront the setbacks of war. He bolted the silver doors of the royal bedroom and sat on the ornate bed. He pondered about a strategic time to use the ultimate weapon to terrify the enemy into submission.

He called out to his dog, needing the comfort of his warmth at this decisive moment. No wagging tail rushed towards him. Instead, at his feet he felt the cold body of his dog, his eyes gazing into eternity, a blissful expression on his face as if he had found his jewel.

The little emperor looked at the dead body in horror. He slumped to the floor and embraced the dog. He wept bitterly, shedding enough tears to quench the thirst of the parched desert.

# The Great Wall

The two empires clashed through the centuries. They fought many wars to claim territories in the frigid, barren land. Soldiers who froze to death in battle were declared martyrs. Those who survived or got away with losing a limb or an eye were decorated with elaborate titles, medals and ribbons and declared heroes.

Off and on, following a fruitless battle, there would be a truce and a new emperor would ascend the throne, or an old one would die.

This was one such time. The aging emperor sent his emissaries to the other side of the great wall to make peace. He thought that it was his last chance to be remembered as a statesman before he died.

The younger militant emperor on the other side also needed an excuse to distract his people from their misery and suffering after battle.

So he agreed. They would have an opening in the fortified wall, though there would still be a metal gate with long sharp spikes at the top. Twice a day this gate would open for a brief period, at dawn, when they would raise their flags, or at dusk, when they would lower them so that a dialogue could begin.

This was a typical day. The sun was about to set. The frenzied crowds had gathered on either side to cheer their soldiers, to show their enemy how strong they were. They did this by raising slogans, shouting themselves hoarse. Fierce looking soldiers marched on either side of the gate. They paraded up and down, in unison, kicking their legs high in the air, stomping feet on the ground with great force, demonstrating how they would crush the enemy. This sent a shocked thrill through the milling crowds.

The shouting grew more agitated, the bugles sounded, and the gate opened while the flags were lowered for the day.

Two of most demonic looking soldiers with a big moustaches and beards marched towards the opening to salute each other, almost like tigers released from cages. They faced each other and looked at their opponent with piercing eyes and raised their arms for a brief instant before the iron- gate was shut across the barrier.

The people shouted and clapped. They loved each instant of this hysterical drama.

Between the pauses of the beating drums and the bugles, nobody noticed the fearless little squirrel that crossed the border back and forth, running between the armoured legs of the sentries, totally carefree.

# Perfection

'Do not excel,' said the monk. 'If you do a job too well many things can go wrong. Be satisfied with 90 percent. Do not aim at doing a job to perfection. In any case only the Buddha is perfect and even about him, who knows?

'If you do a job well, you will arouse envy and jealousy. You will lose friends; people will grow bitter towards you. Complete a job to perfection, but almost. This way people will be able to criticize your mistakes and feel superior — at the same time the job you have done will function well. Above all, by not demanding perfection, your ego will remain calm balanced and you will be happy. A job executed perfectly can be unhealthy for the person doing it even if he controls his ego.

'Let me tell you about a master carpenter. Without a job, he came to a new city. He went to a rich landlord and asked for a place to stay. The landlord in a moment of generosity gave him a deserted, broken down shack to stay in.

'The master craftsman, being what he was, immediately started working on the shack. He carved the wood intricately. From the old planks he re-crafted the little shack to a perfect structure.

'The landlord, on one of his outings over his vast estate, saw this beautiful structure and was amazed at the sight. He met the carpenter and told him to stay in the ramshackle building behind it. He wanted the new structure for himself.

'The carpenter started working on the deserted house again. This time it took another graceful form.

'The landlord saw the transformed building the following month and said: "I want this house for my friend. You will need to move into the place behind."'

Being a perfectionist, the carpenter sweated and sweated. Nail by nail, he worked, day and night, till he had built himself an architectural masterpiece.

'It cannot be true. This is a mirage, a building of such magnificence, and on my land. Why, if I rent it out, I will be a millionaire! Get out of here. I want this building now,' he told the carpenter.

There were no more desolate structures on his land for the carpenter to stay in. The perfectionist trudged through the city alone – homeless, once again.

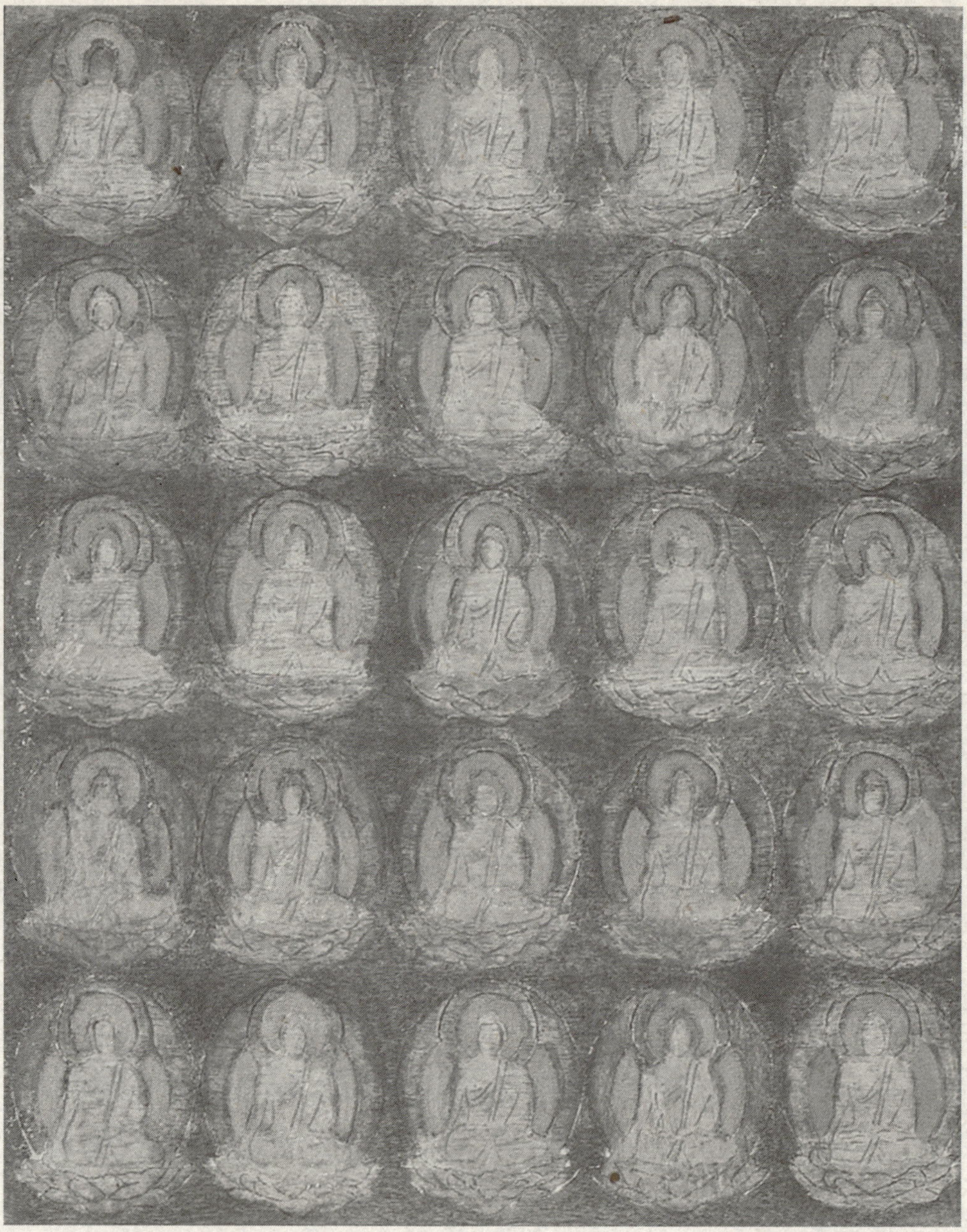

# Enough

The monk kept chanting the mantra on and on. He had taken a vow that he would chant it a million times at a stretch thinking that this would surely please the Buddha. And he would be a step closer to him.

This went on for hours, days and weeks. He became an object of attention for all the monks and devotees at the monastery. In the process, he neglected his duties. The mundane tasks at the monastery were beneath his dignity. He was seeking something higher, something spiritually uplifting.

He sat in one spot, did not eat or drink and kept repeating the mantra. The other monks, keeping track of his prayers, too became involved...fifty thousand... sixty thousand... seventy thousand. Some of them even joined the chanting, as they kept the score.

The crowds that came to see this wonder grew larger and larger, the peace and tranquillity of the monastery was totally disrupted. This drama soon became a nuisance, but people loved it.

The monk was enjoying it all. He basked in the glory of his outstanding act. Soon, another monk started chanting a more powerful mantra and he vowed to beat him by chanting it two million times. A younger monk took the cue and said that he would outdo them both and would chant the mantra five million times. There was chaos. Groups were formed with acolytes backing different monks. Life changed completely at the monastery as people waited for the first monk to reach his goal.

'Ninety nine thousand, nine hundred and ninety nine...' someone shouted at the top of his voice.

'Enough' whispered the roshi from the sanctum sanctorum. The counting stopped. There was hushed silence.

'Enough' repeated the roshi. 'Have you all forgotten the first lesson that life has taught us? I waited quietly all this time and did not stop you earlier from this useless endeavour so that you would realize its futility yourself. Look at what you have achieved. It was your task to feed the hungry and take care of the elderly. They have been neglected and are sick. This place is a mess, water has not been collected from the stream, the plants are withering, the roof tiles have not been replaced and we will soon freeze in the coming cold wave.

'Do you think that the Buddha will be pleased by hearing his name a million times and shower you with his benevolence, or would he rather you took care of the things that are meaningful? Chanting and praying are very important, but things carried to excess become destructive.

'It is of utmost importance to know when to say enough.

'Suppose a sculptor made a magnificent sculpture and reached a state of perfection but kept chiselling and hammering away at the stone. What would happen if he did not know when to say enough? Or the mother kept pampering the child and never let the child grow up and be on its own?

'The list is endless and can go all the way up to the most powerful leader. The leader, by not knowing when he has enough power, leads to his own downfall.

'Only nature is not like that. In spite of the seeming excesses, it never forgets the first lesson - balance is ever present because nature always remembers when "enough is enough."'

125

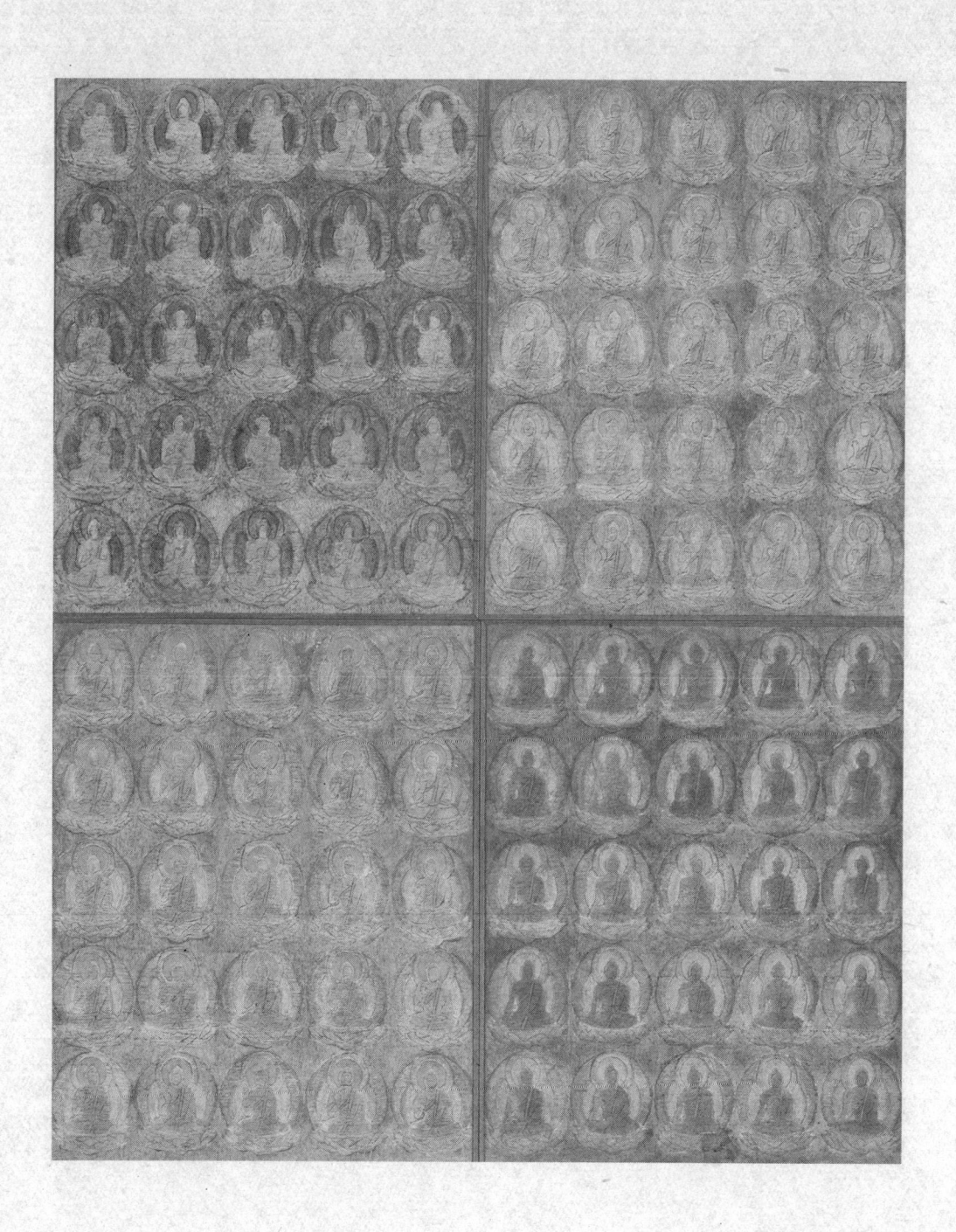

# Exhale

My roshi, while teaching us a new set of martial art movements, said, 'Exhale...and the inhalation will take care of itself.'

Such a simple direct instruction, but how difficult it is to understand and adhere to, I thought.

The roshi continued, 'Through most of our lives we inhale and inhale, while forgetting to exhale. We take in, accumulate and store more and more baggage. We load ourselves with food that does not nourish us. We gather objects we have no use for, hoard money we may never be able to enjoy. We fill not just our lungs, but our being with polluted air, leaving no room for the breath of fresh air which could give us energy, which could sustain our lives.'

And then coming behind me the grand master said, 'Now stretch your arms upwards and as you come down to touch your feet, exhale deeply.'

'No, no, exhale from your gut, not just from your throat.'

And I thought of the last time that I gave away something that was dear to me - my silk robe. It was difficult. Was I just exhaling from the throat? I resolved to be tougher with myself. I planned to clean out my cupboard, not just the cupboard, but my home of all the unnecessary objects before I went for the next session.

I kept just a minimal number of clothes, a blanket, a mattress and some utensils to cook my food. Only the rare wooden statue of Buddha and my library of books, I retained.

The roshi would understand, I thought. It was knowledge that I was keeping for myself, the sacred treasure that I had to keep for posterity, I reasoned.

When I went for the next marital arts session, I was very pleased with myself for having understood and followed the grand master's instructions. Then, as if reading my mind he said, 'Burn the books, and as for the Buddha's statue you may use it for firewood…with the snow falling, its getting a little chilly, isn't it?'

I was shocked. How could the roshi ask me to commit such an outrageous and sacrilegious act?

'Exhale! You are still exhaling from your chest and not from your gut,' said the roshi

It took many painful days and sleepless nights to understand what he said further. 'Knowledge is not acquired by just reading the books. They can be a great burden because you may just start parroting all the wise sayings, quote from the sutras without understanding the real meaning. Or repeating the mantras in the ancient language and feel very superior to others who do not understand the language.

'The thing of value is what you have retained, what you have truly comprehended from all the written texts.

'The same goes for the rare Buddha statue. If a man is freezing to death, Buddha would be only too happy to be used as firewood to save his life.'

I gave away my books and the statue and my last possessions to a monastery nearby. Unburdened, I was floating in the air, when I went for the next session at the dojo, the training area. This was going to be a very tough and a rigorous session. But I was elated with the thought that the roshi would be very happy with my action.

'Don't kick your legs in the air so hard. Relax. Don't throw your opponent down with such vengeance. You are still clinging to the thought of your accomplishment.

'Exhale deeply from your gut, exhale till it becomes your second nature - your very being.'

'Exhale!' is all he said.

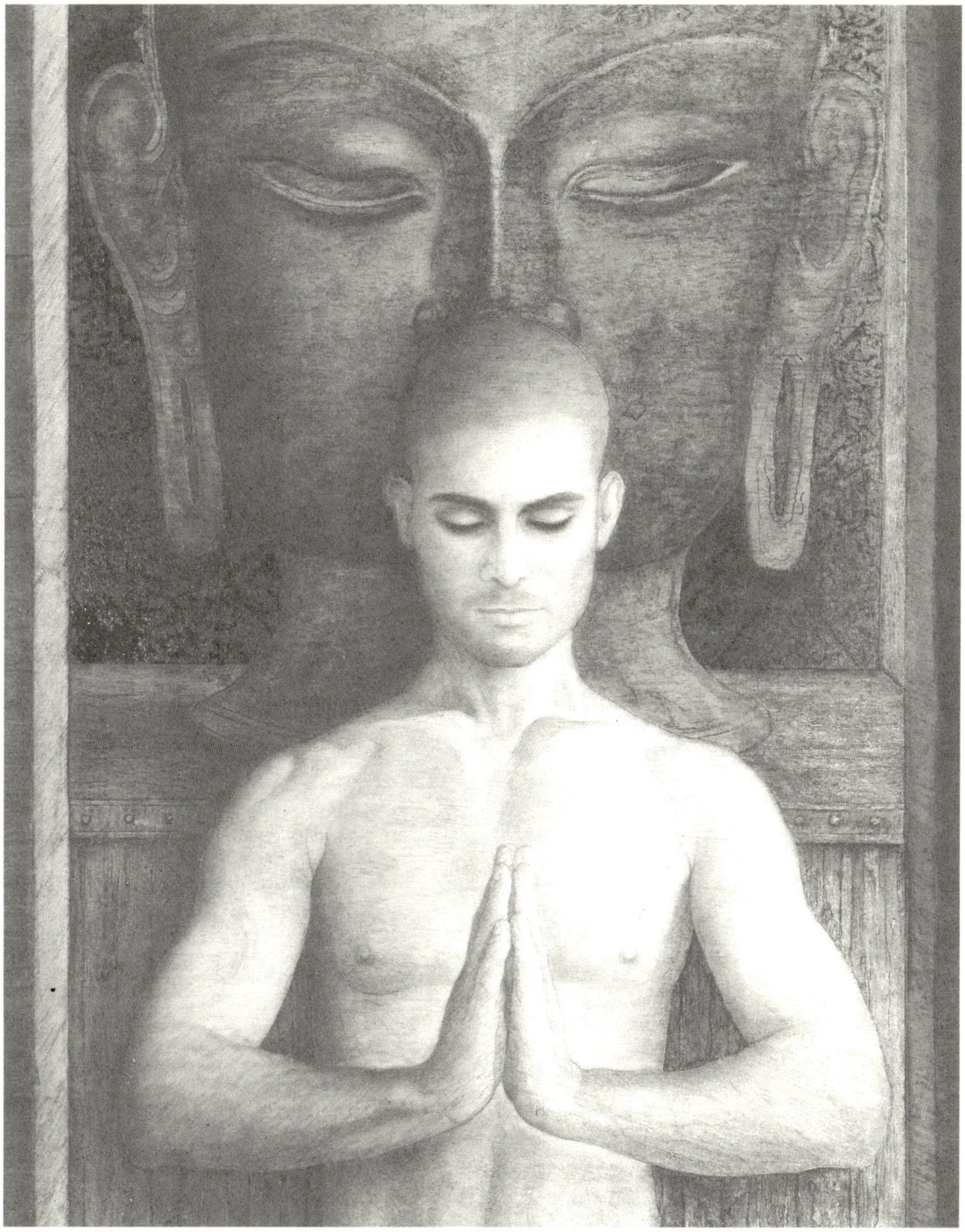

# Fleeting Moments

*Insights and Reflections*

# Boundaries

*This new
bamboo shoot
hangs over
my neighbour's wall
– it hasn't yet learned
about boundaries.*

# The Search

*Many, many paths
lead to Buddha
But the steps are
a bit slippery.*

# Impermanence

*Between life
and death
just one breath,
and yet, an eternity.*

# Grudges

*Water hardens into ice
– a little warmth
and it melts.*

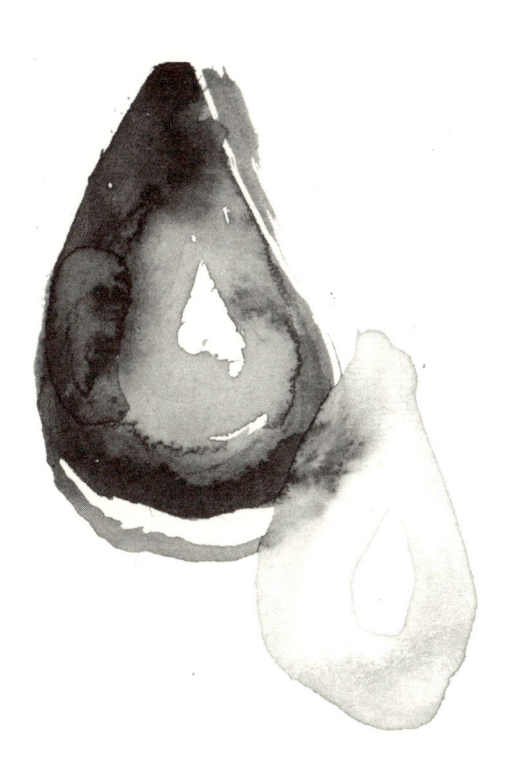

# Destiny

*Five new shoots
in my bamboo grove...
Five sticks or
five brushes?*

# Fate

*Does the wave before
dissolving on the shore,
question its destiny?*

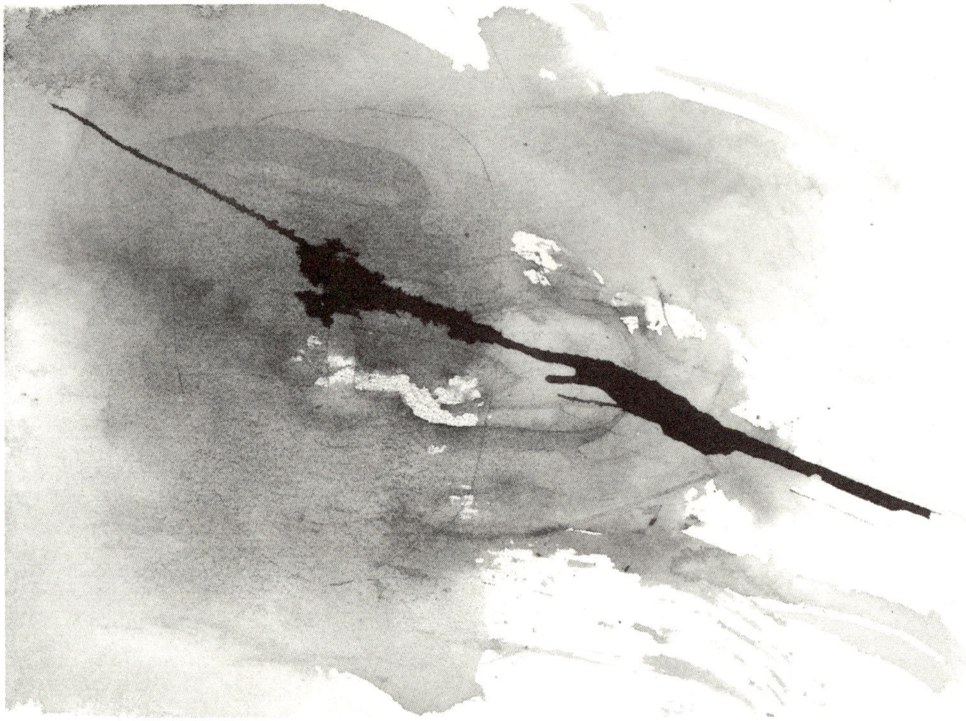

# Single-mindedness

*The crow flying straight*
*to its destination*
*missed seeing*
*all the wildflowers.*

# Hesitation

*The potter's wheel stopped to think, and ceased to be a wheel.*

# Discontent

*Calm sea, just one piece,*
*of jigsaw washed ashore,*
*– the puzzle begins*

# Breaking Free

*Only when the dandelion*
*gave up dreaming*
*of immortality*
*did it become free.*

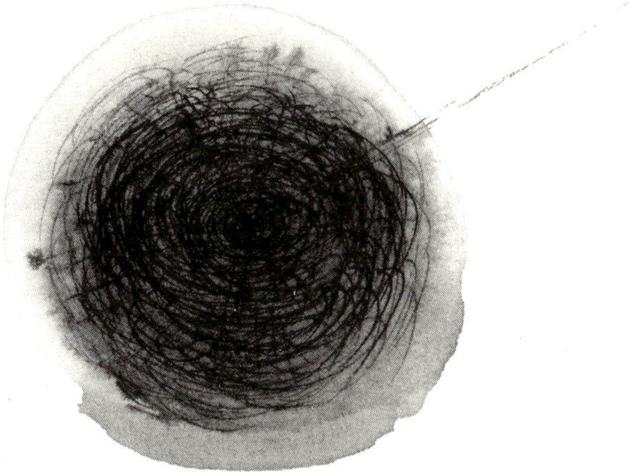

# Entrapped

*A single wildflower,
enough to obscure
my view of the
pristine mountain.*

# Disclosure

*Mist clad valley,
the sound of a bell ringing
in the monastery,
the monks can't
hide their presence.*

# Arrogance

*Not used to having
its yoke lifted,
the bull feels
insecure.*

# Fortune

*On a dry summer day,
which is better?
Counting money or
counting raindrops?*

# Envy

*Two butterflies,
envious of each other's
wings compared their
intricate patterns
while an unadorned white
one fluttered by.*

# Fortitude

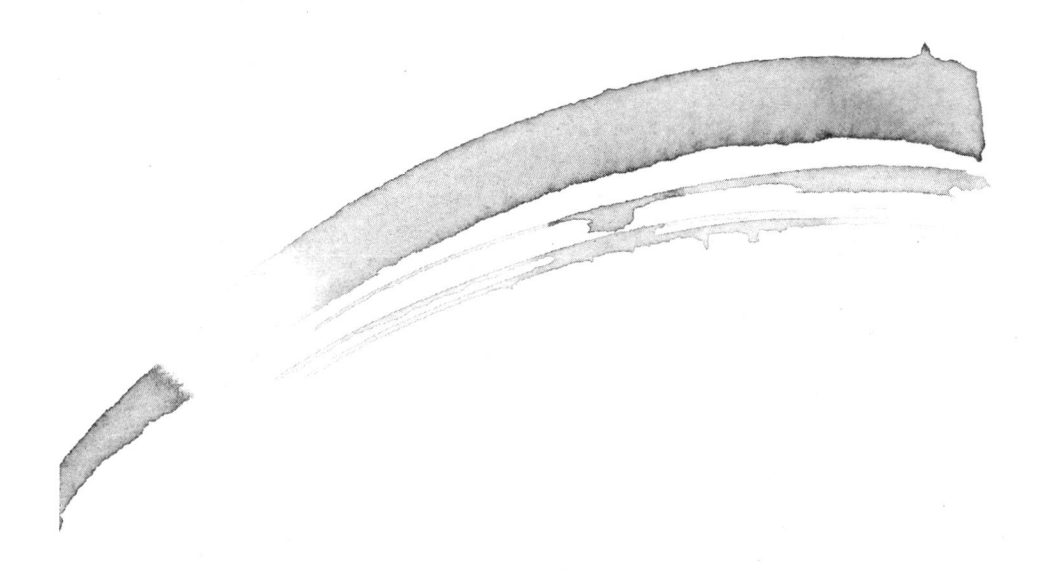

*However hard they try
thunderclouds cannot
wash away the colour
from the rainbow,
It shines even brighter.*

# Struggle

*There must be a way*
*out of this maze*
*– the open sky*

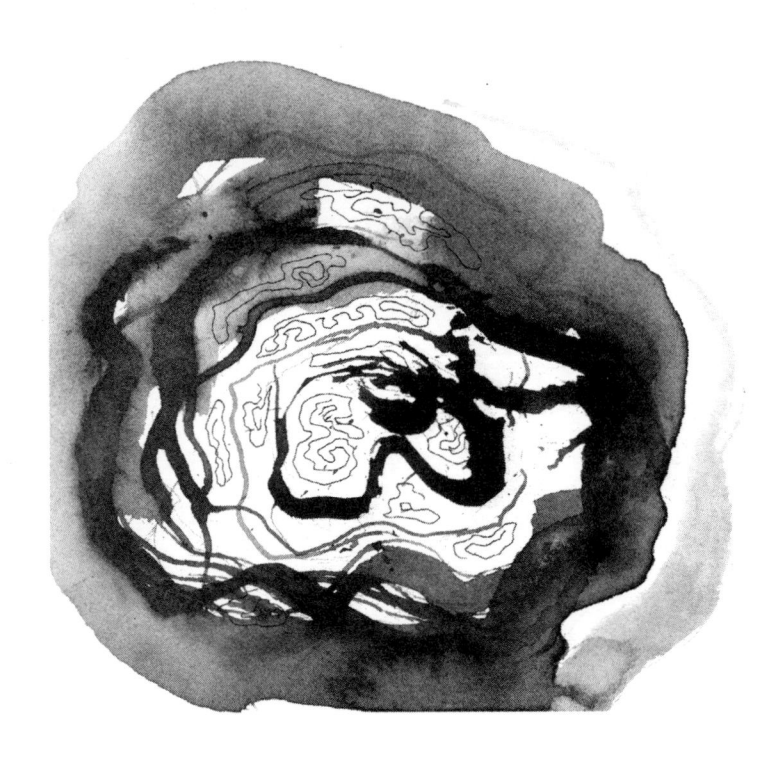

# Reassurance

*Each time my lantern flickers, I look up at the flickering stars.*

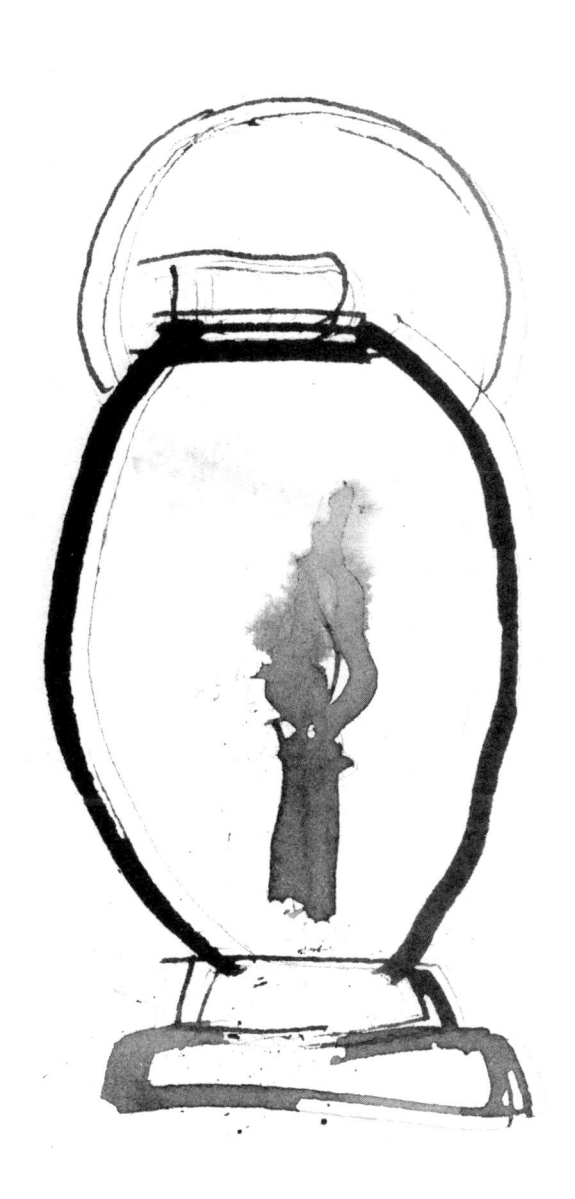

# Perception

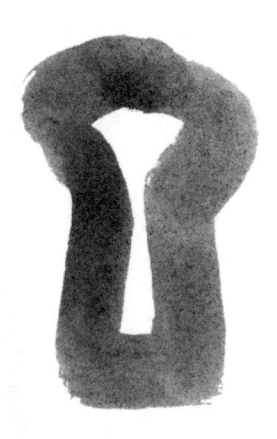

*We have our fortune
with us all the time,
but, often, misplace
the key.*

# Possession

*Our love solid as
a rock,
but the stones
are cold.*

# Saviour ?

*After praying
to the gilded Buddha
for protection,
they locked him away
behind iron bars.*

155

# Karma

*The stronger the stone
thrown into the water,
the larger, the ripple.*

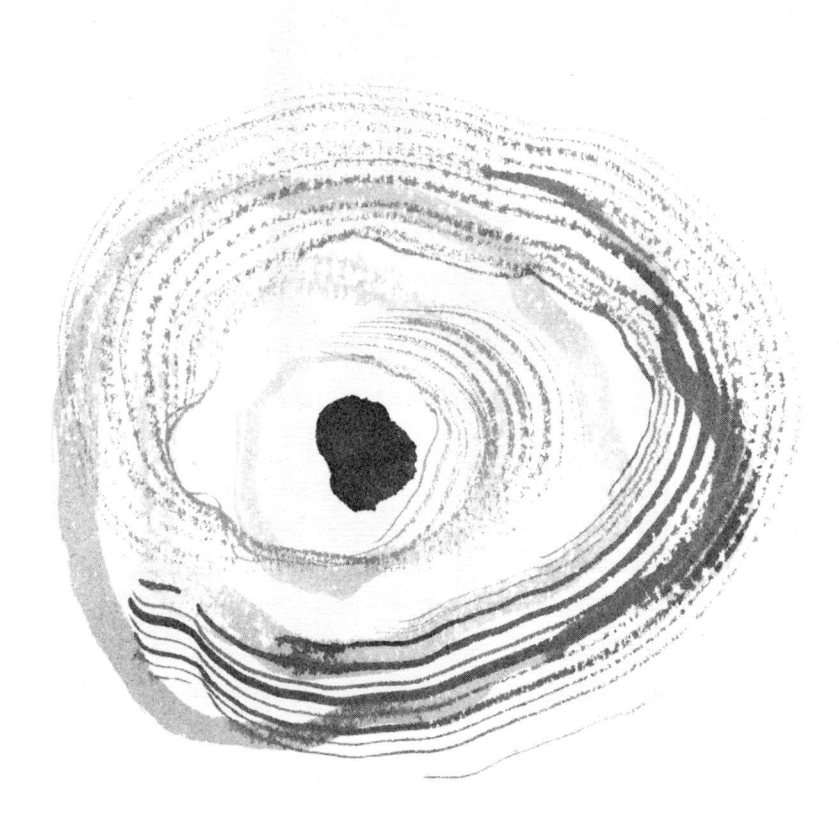

# Spark

*Smoke rising from
the hearth,
smoke spreading from
a forest fire
— what a difference.*

# Thank You

My grateful thanks to His Holiness the Dalai Lama, for showing me the way.

Many thanks to Amita, my soul mate for sharing this life with me; Ayesha, my dear friend for being a part of the initial awakening; Bharat, for giving me the opportunity to express my thoughts; to Karen, for helping me with the first draft; to Harsha, my publisher and finally to Anupa, my editor for being merciless with the scissors.